How to Draw Unicorns For Kids Gift

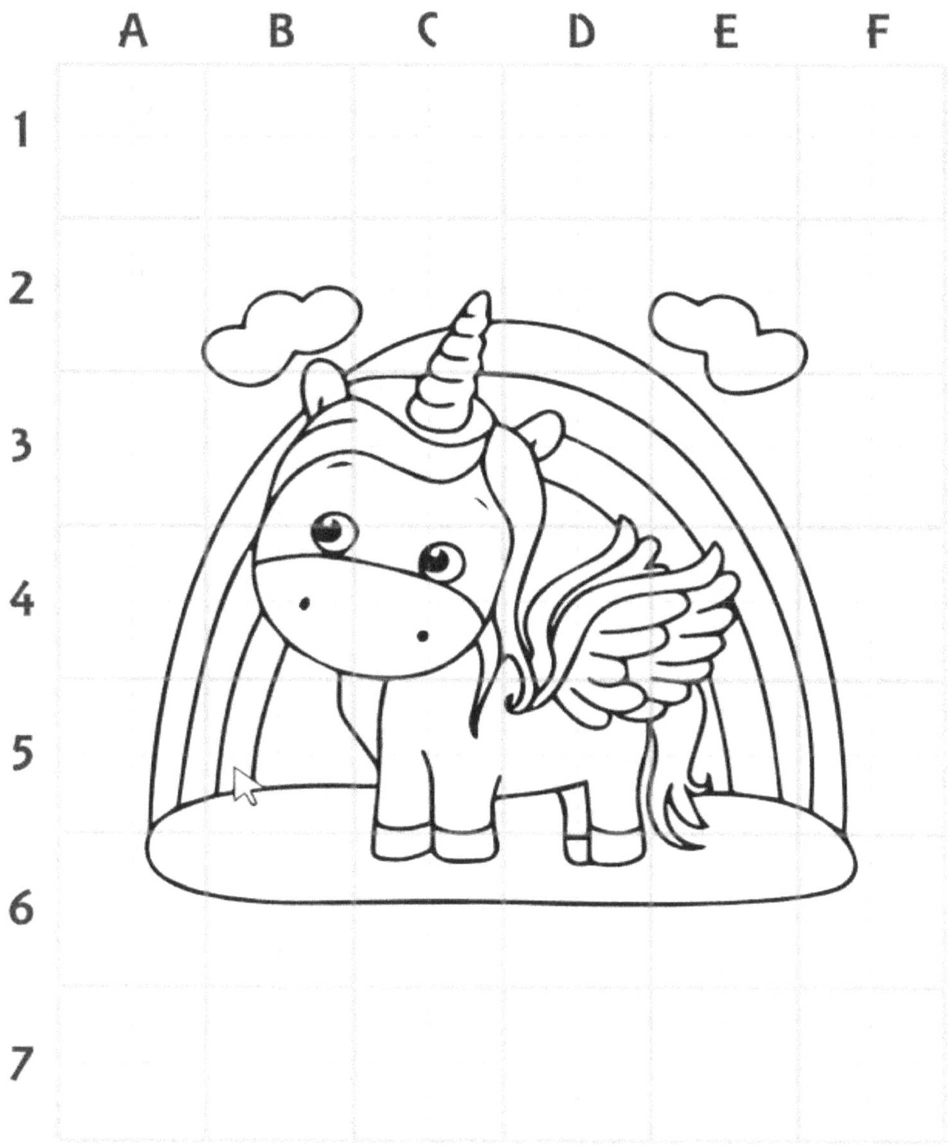

This Sketchbook Belongs To

SA BOOK HOUSE

WRITE US TO RECEIVE A GIFT FOR YOUR CHILD AS SOON AS YOU HAVE PURCHASED OUR BOOK

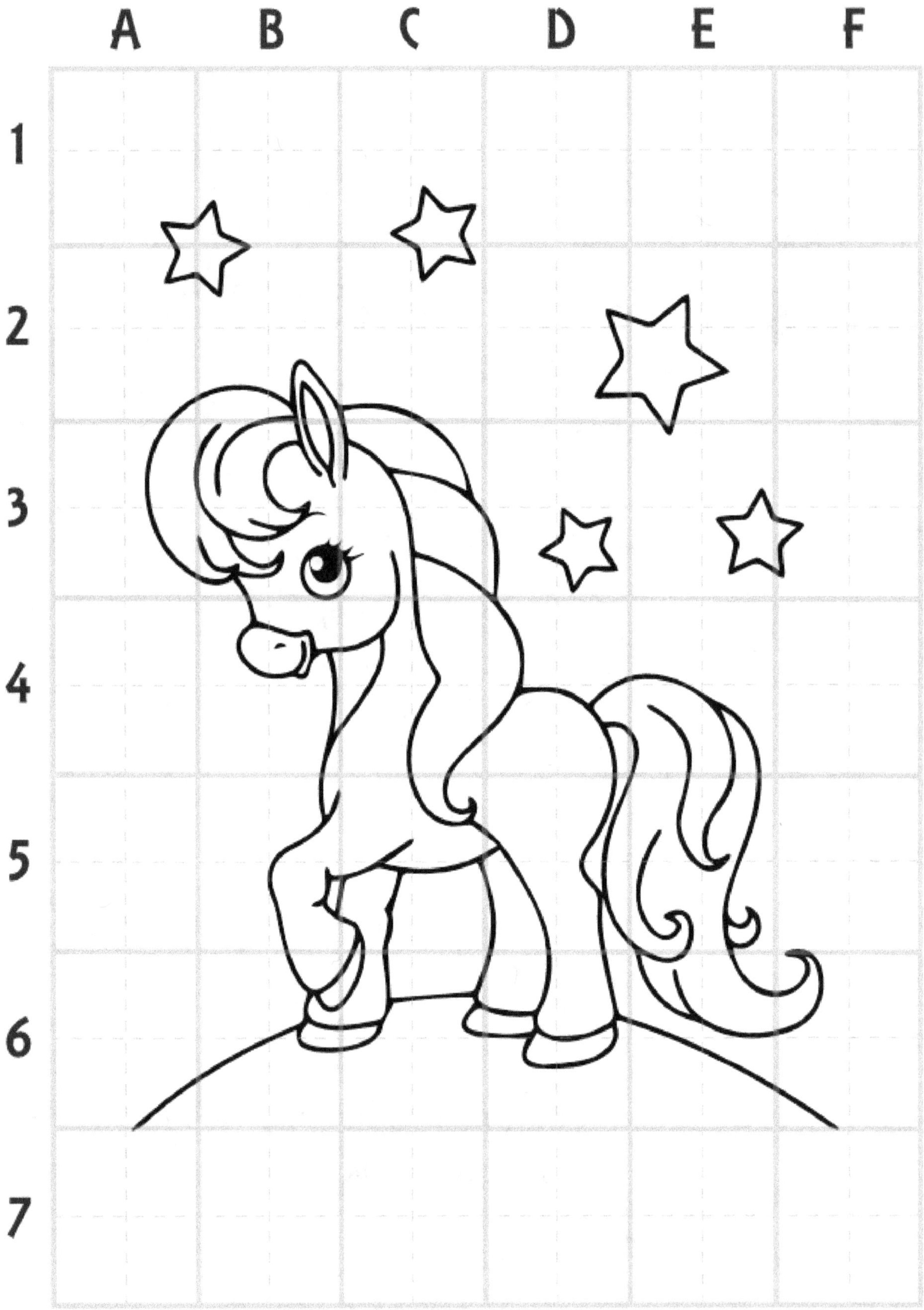
A
B
C
D
E
F
1
2
3
4
5
6
7

YOUR TURN!

	A	B	C	D	E	F
1						
2						
3						
4						
5						
6						
7						

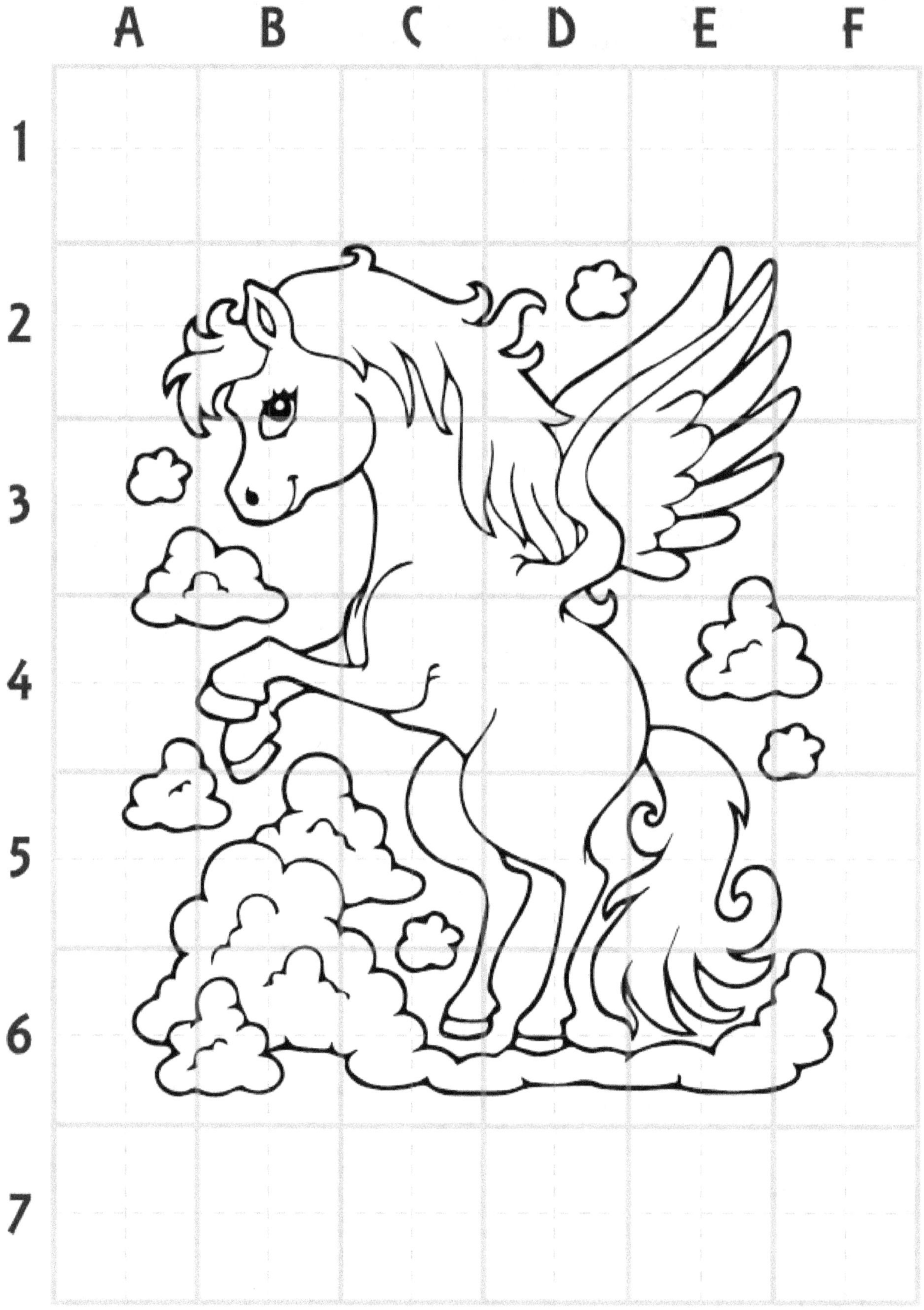
A B C D E F
1 2 3 4 5 6 7

YOUR TURN!

	A	B	C	D	E	F
1						
2						
3						
4						
5						
6						
7						

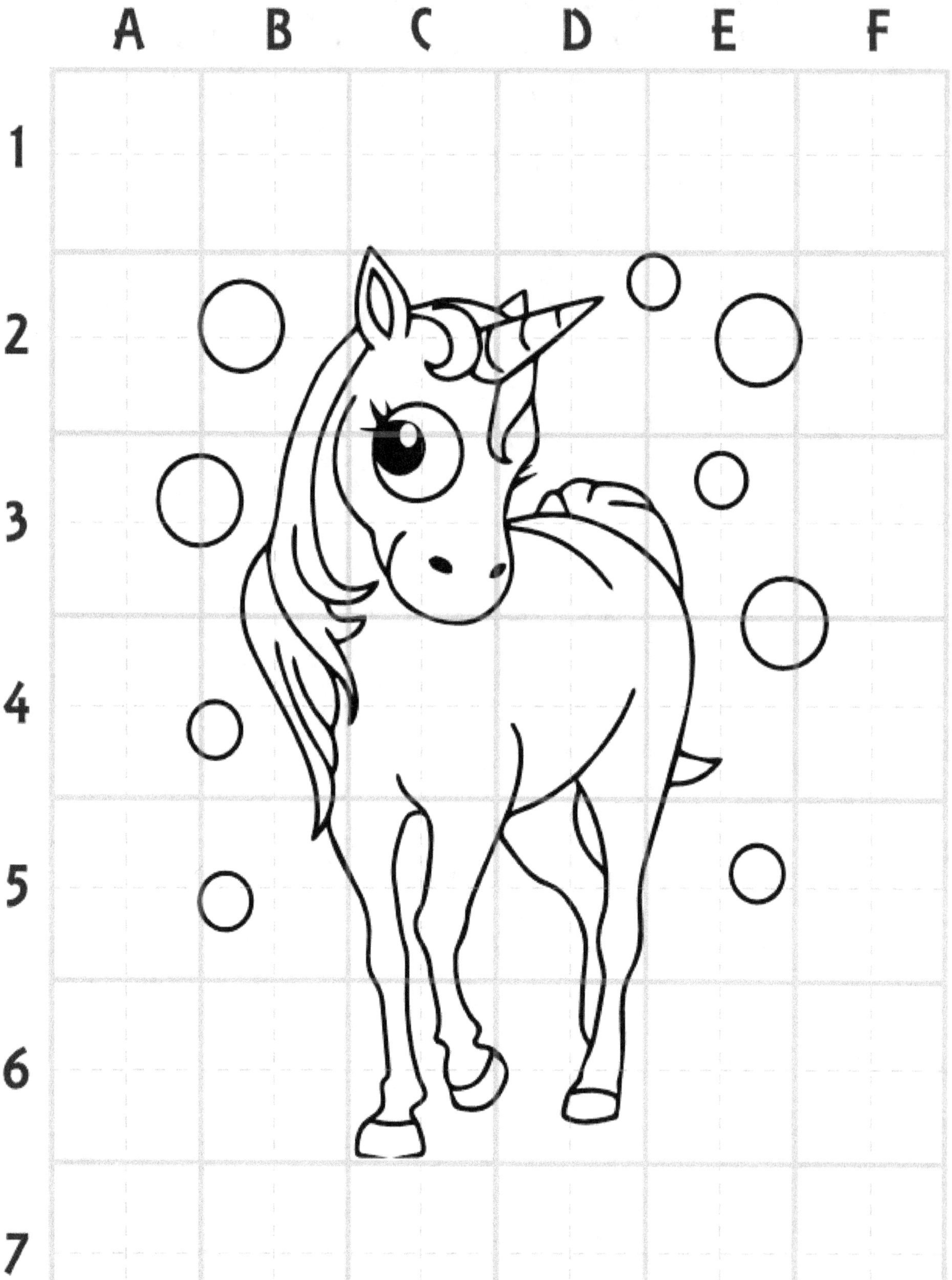
A
B
C
D
E
F
1
2
3
4
5
6
7

YOUR TURN!

	A	B	C	D	E	F
1						
2						
3						
4						
5						
6						
7						

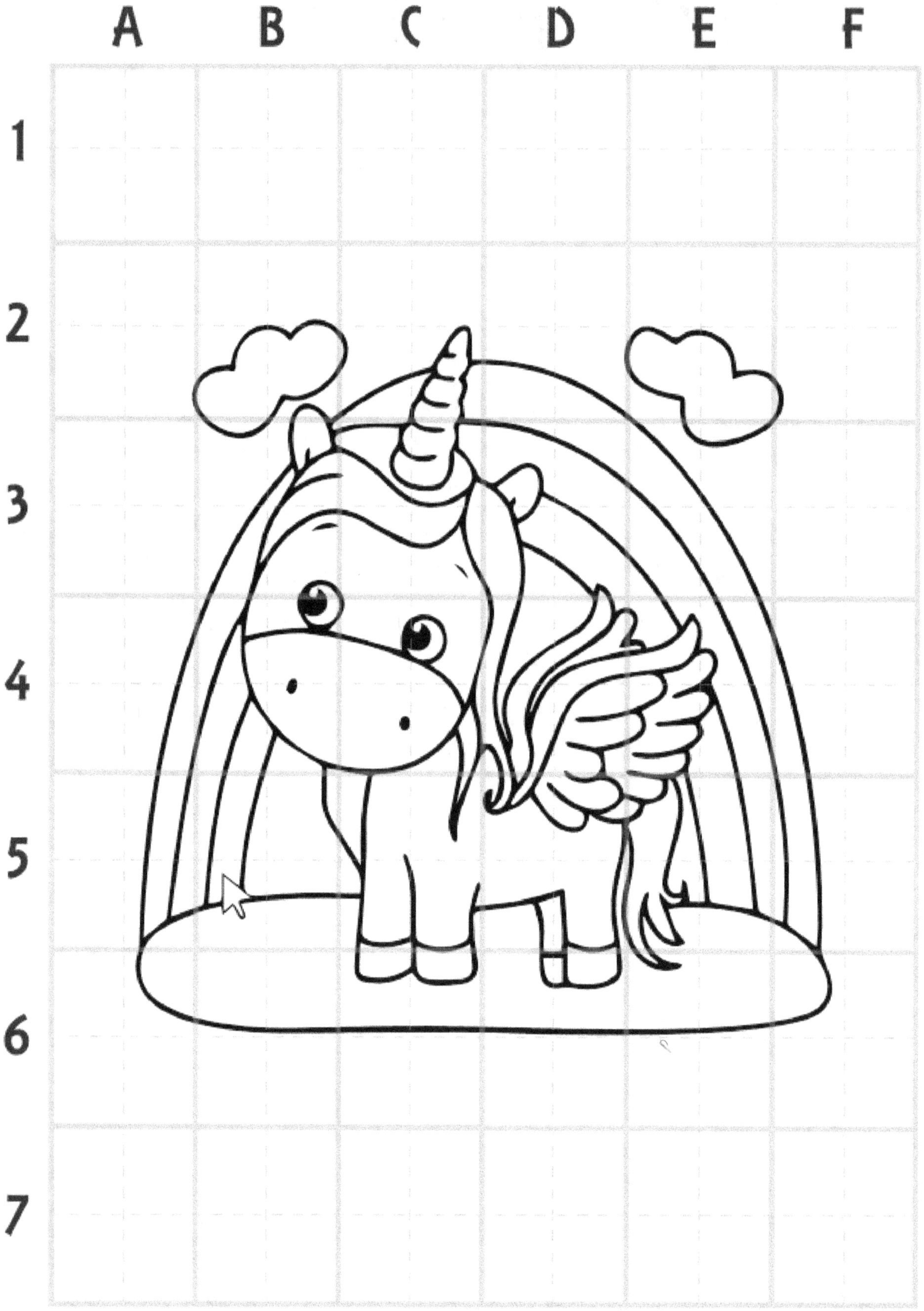
A B C D E F
1
2
3
4
5
6
7

YOUR TURN!

	A	B	C	D	E	F
1						
2						
3						
4						
5						
6						
7						

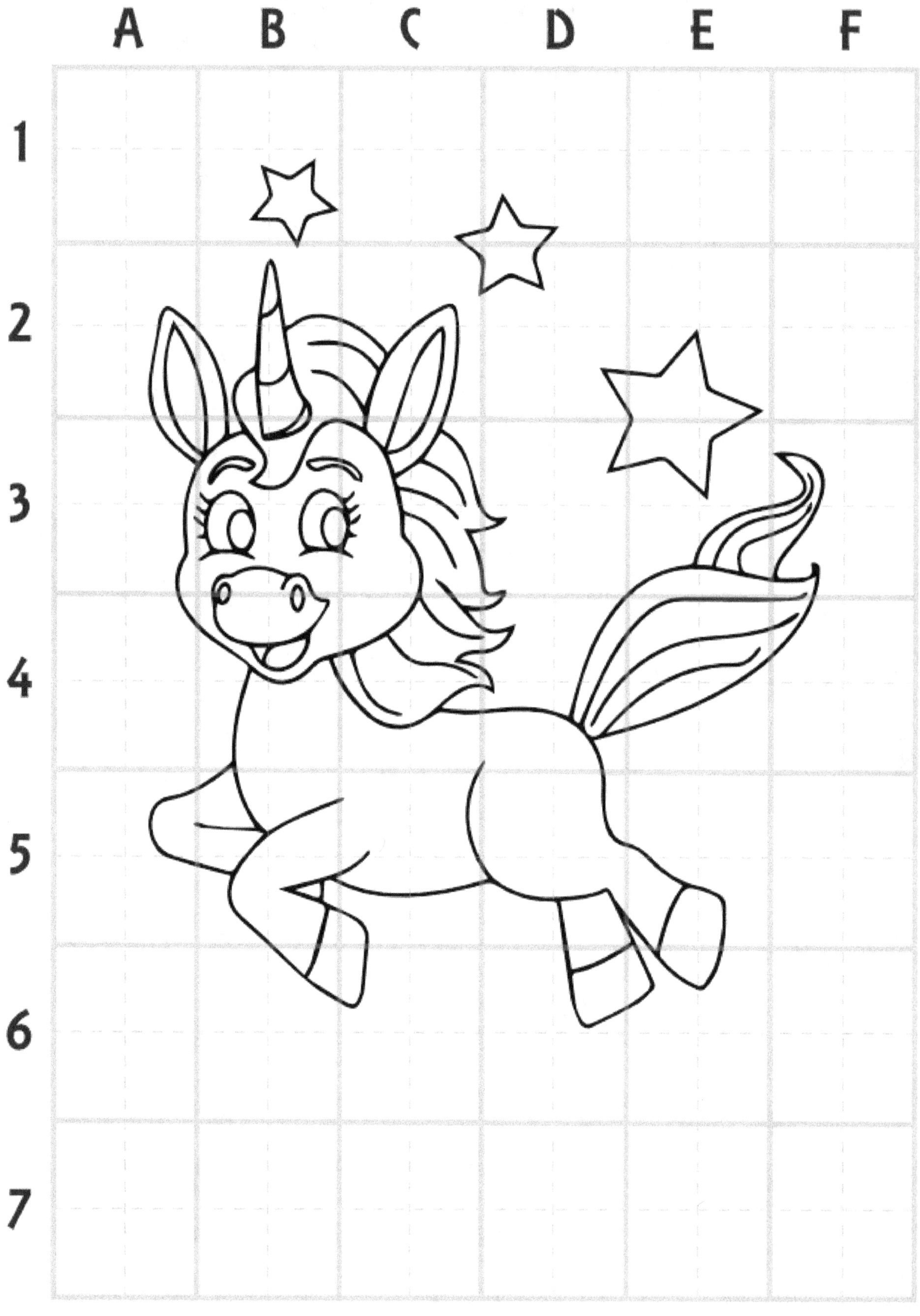
A
B
C
D
E
F
1
2
3
4
5
6
7

YOUR TURN!

	A	B	C	D	E	F
1						
2						
3						
4						
5						
6						
7						

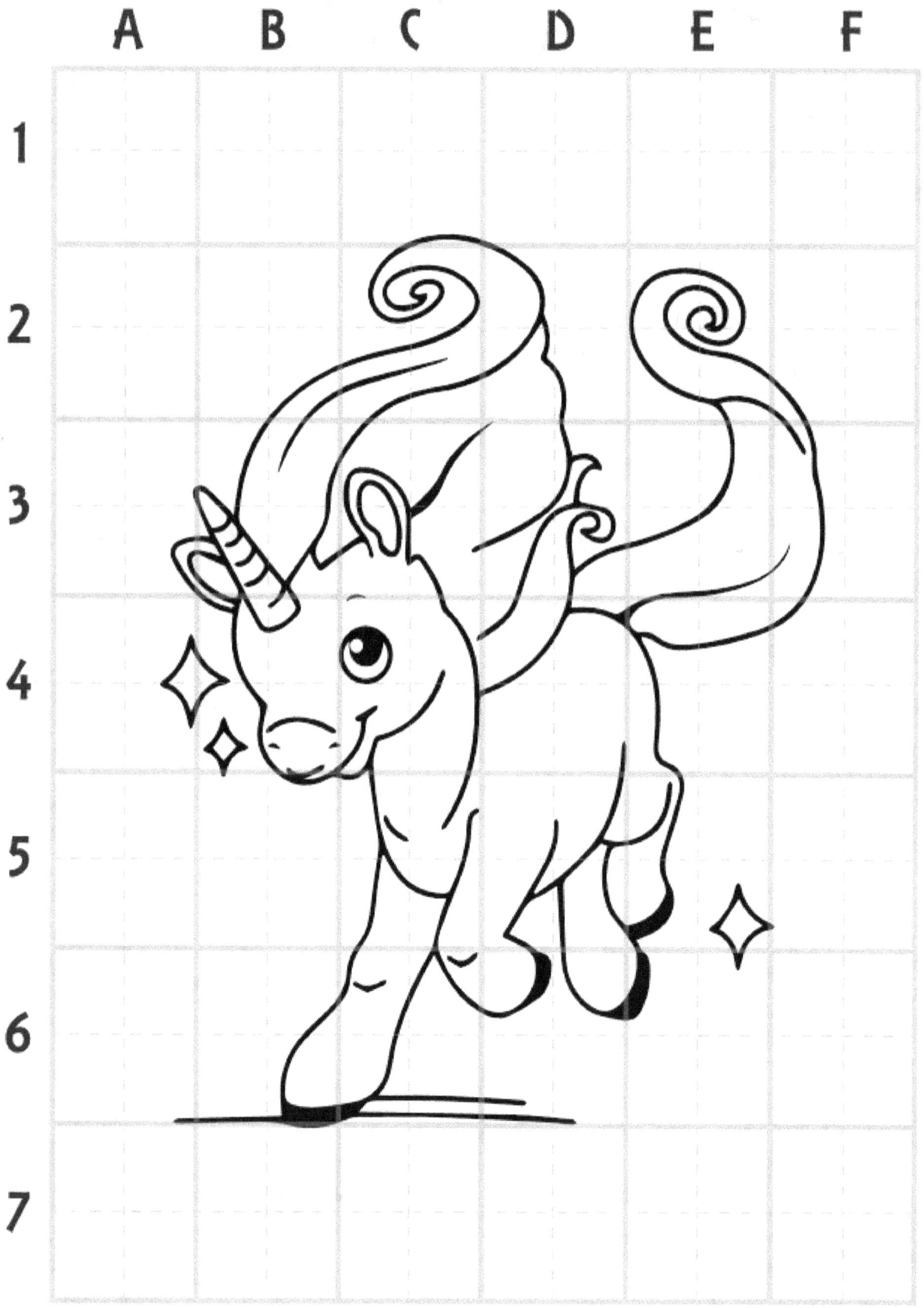
A B C D E F
1
2
3
4
5
6
7

YOUR TURN!

	A	B	C	D	E	F
1						
2						
3						
4						
5						
6						
7						

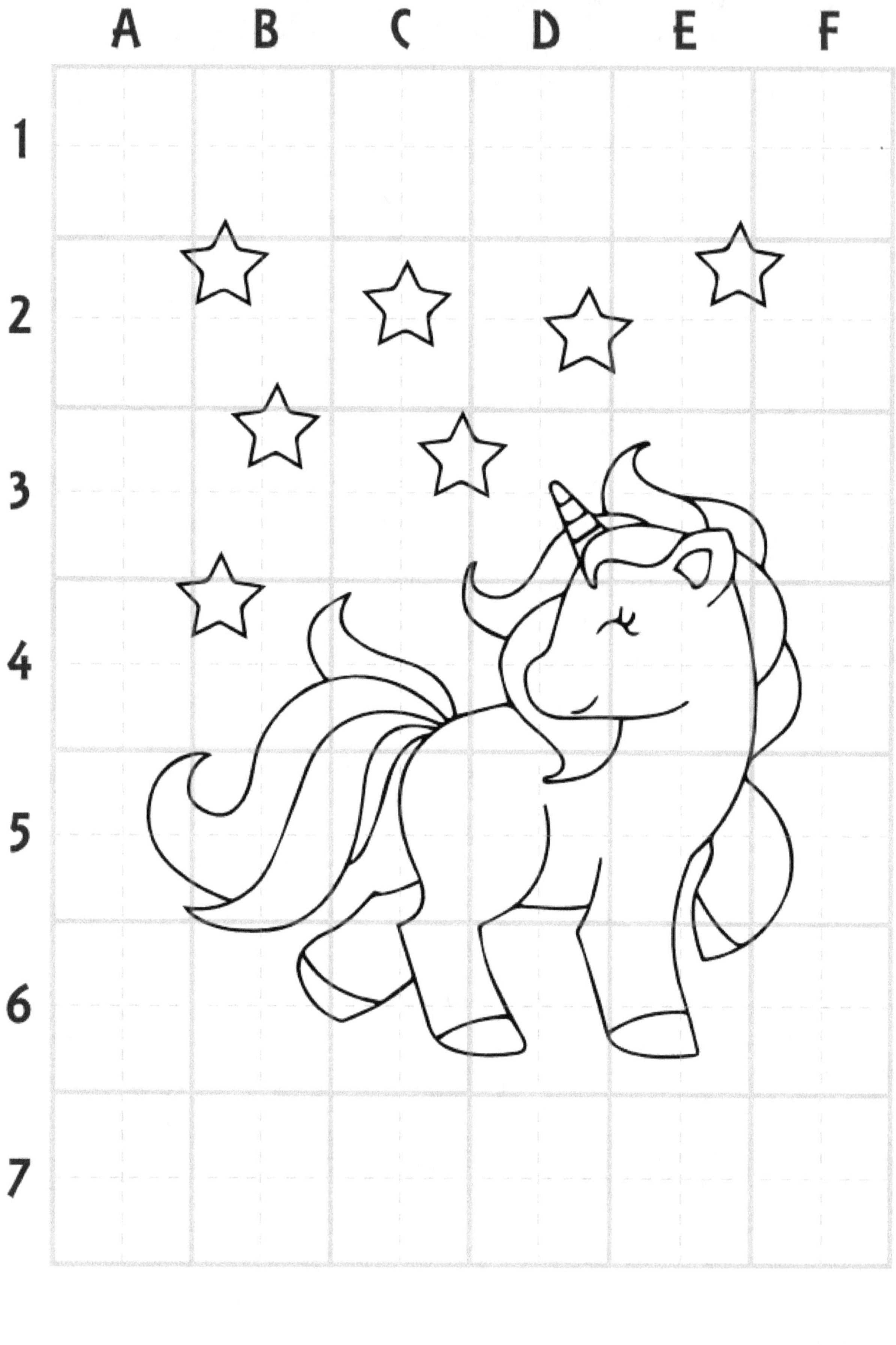
A B C D E F
1
2
3
4
5
6
7

YOUR TURN!

	A	B	C	D	E	F
1						
2						
3						
4						
5						
6						
7						

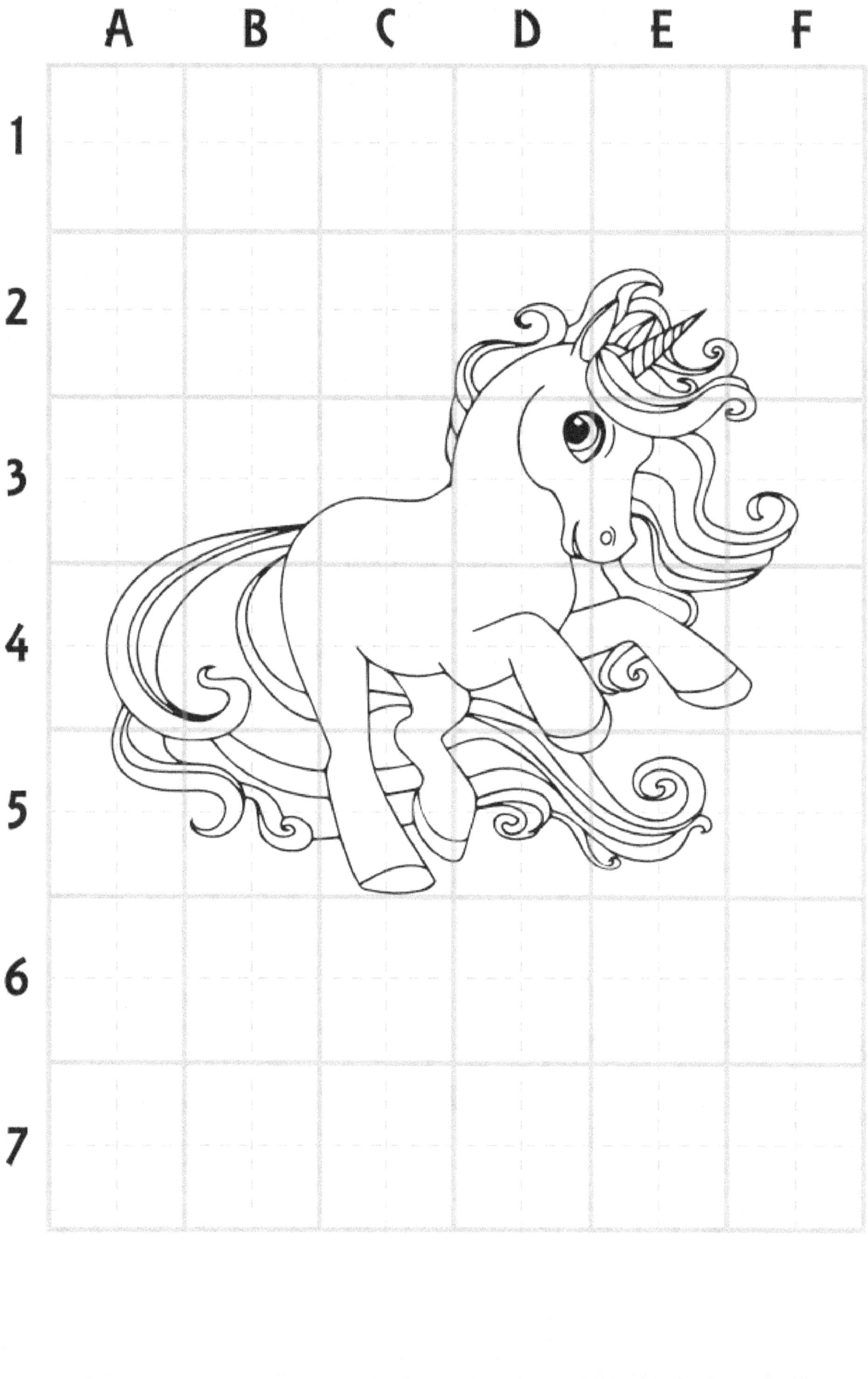
A B C D E F
1
2
3
4
5
6
7

YOUR TURN!

	A	B	C	D	E	F
1						
2						
3						
4						
5						
6						
7						

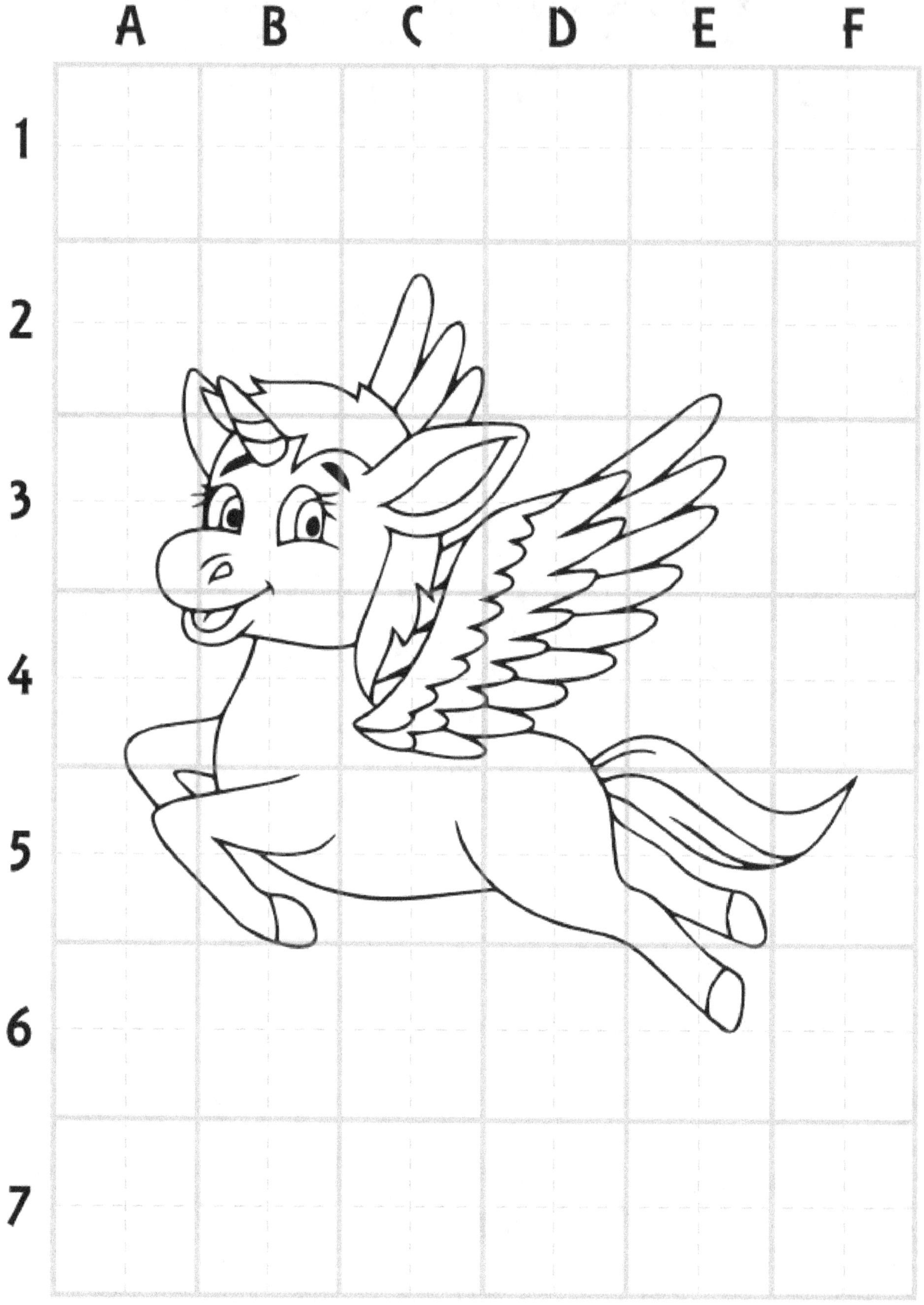
A
B
C
D
E
F
1
2
3
4
5
6
7

YOUR TURN!

	A	B	C	D	E	F
1						
2						
3						
4						
5						
6						
7						

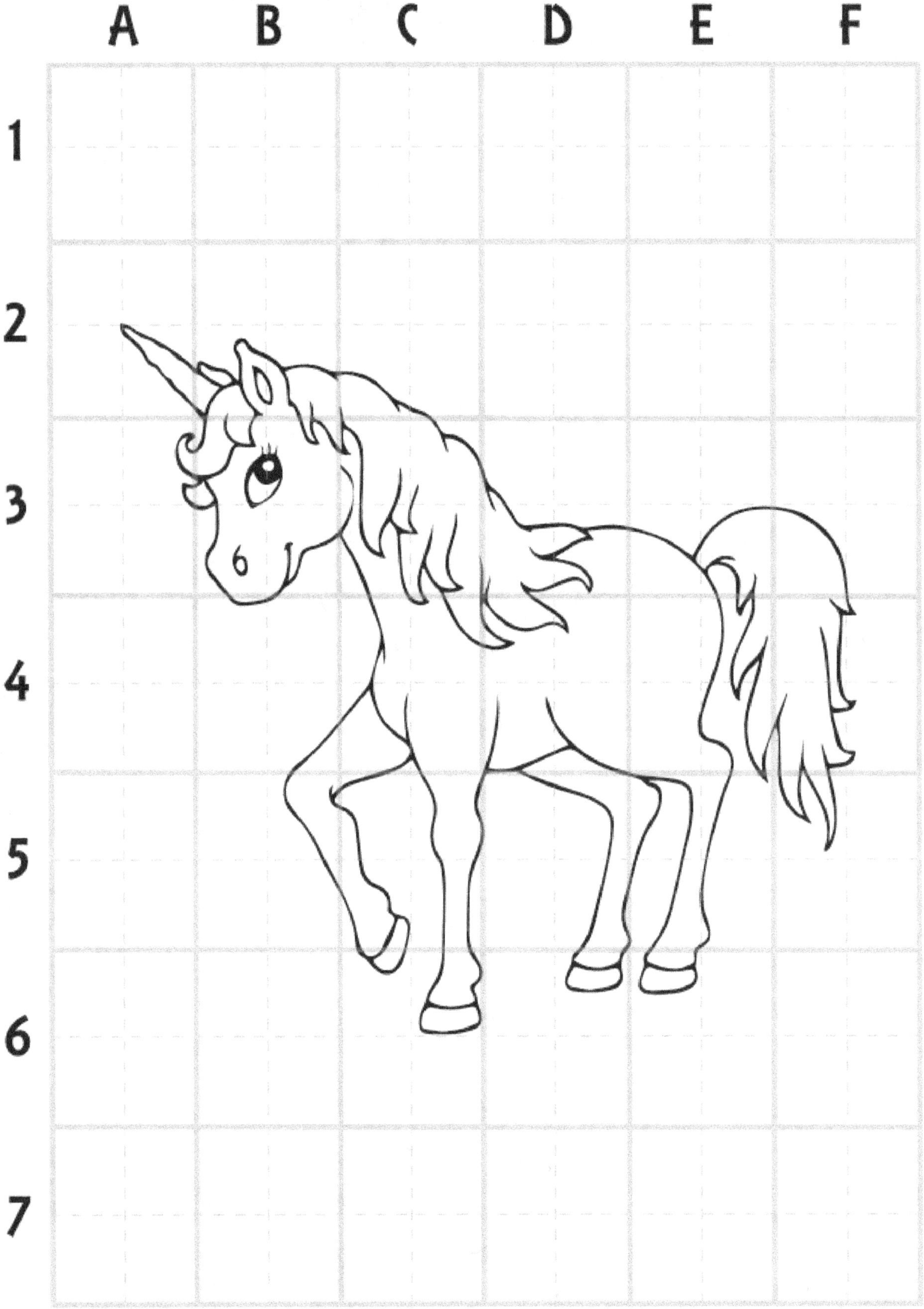
A
B
C
D
E
F
1
2
3
4
5
6
7

YOUR TURN!

	A	B	C	D	E	F
1						
2						
3						
4						
5						
6						
7						

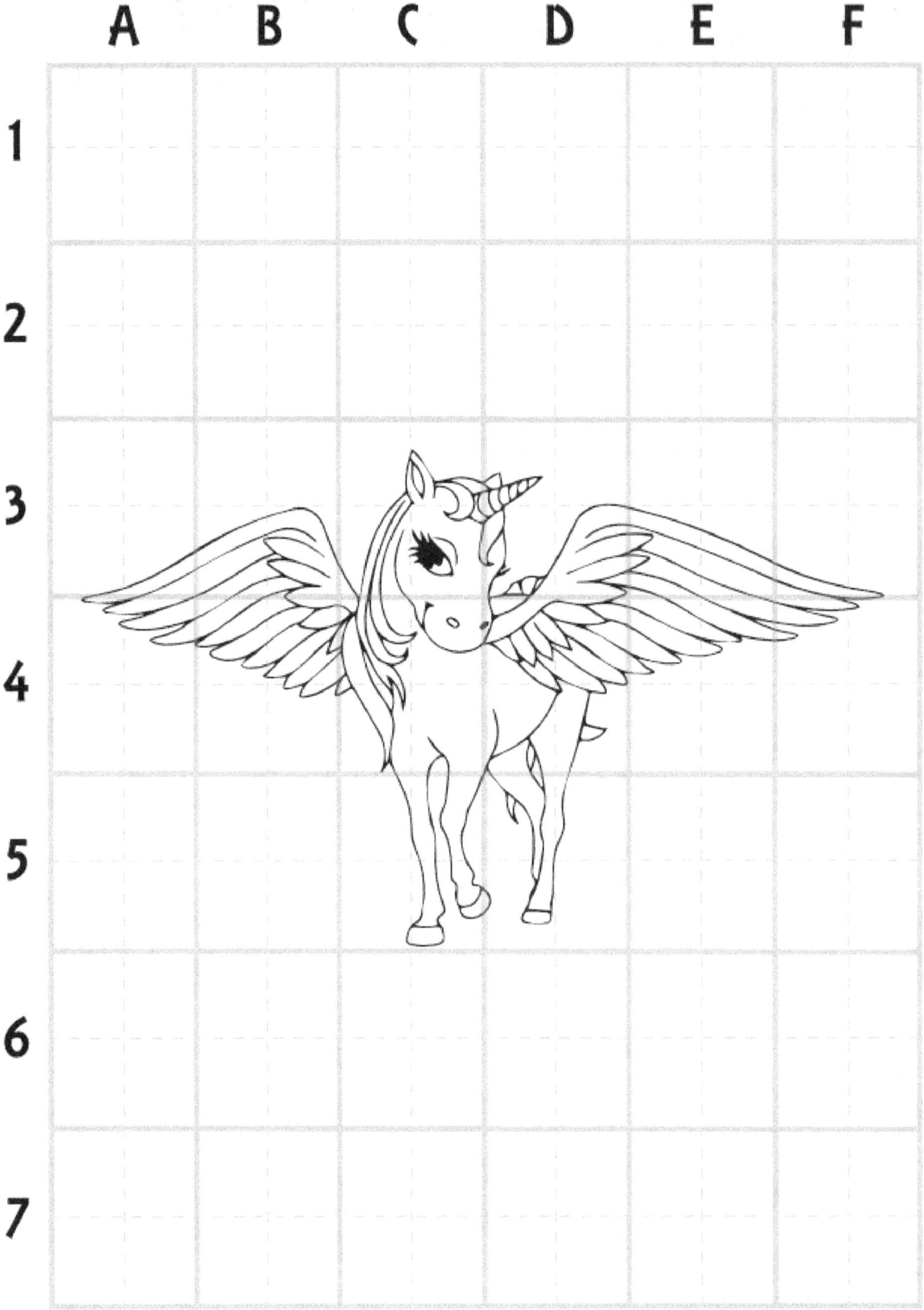
A
B
C
D
E
F
1
2
3
4
5
6
7

YOUR TURN!

	A	B	C	D	E	F
1						
2						
3						
4						
5						
6						
7						

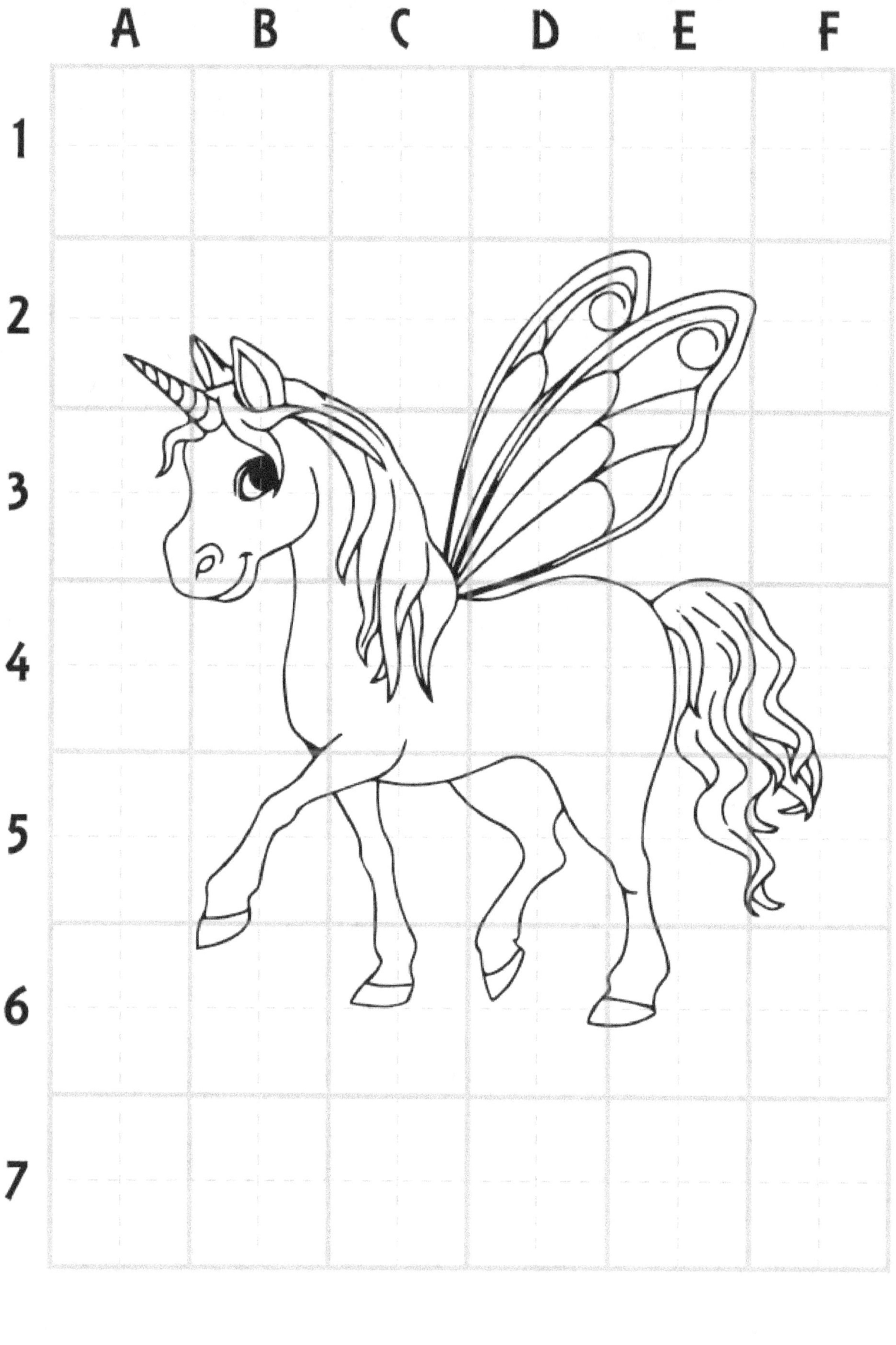
A
B
C
D
E
F
1
2
3
4
5
6
7

YOUR TURN!

	A	B	C	D	E	F
1						
2						
3						
4						
5						
6						
7						

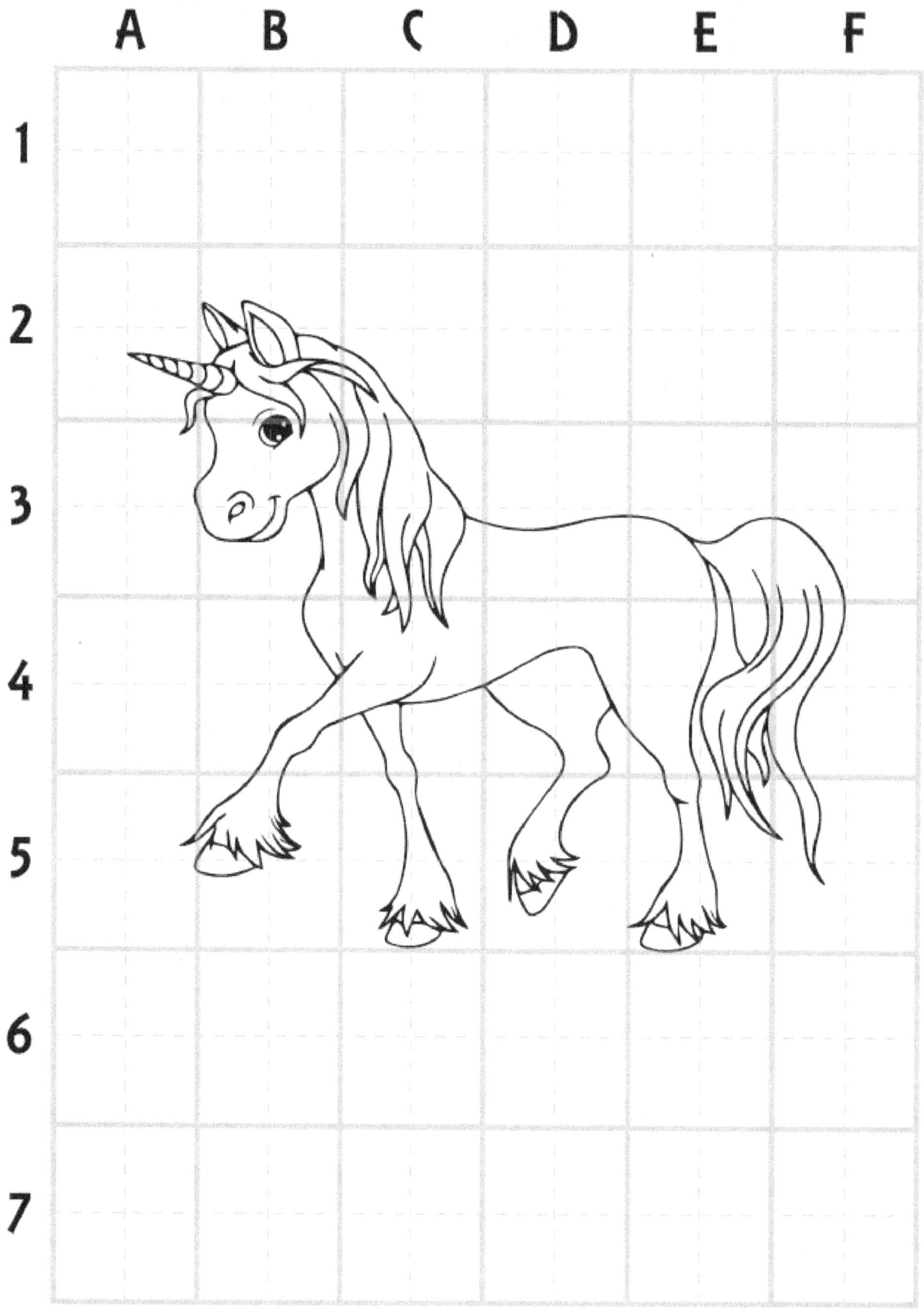
A
B
C
D
E
F
1
2
3
4
5
6
7

YOUR TURN!

	A	B	C	D	E	F
1						
2						
3						
4						
5						
6						
7						

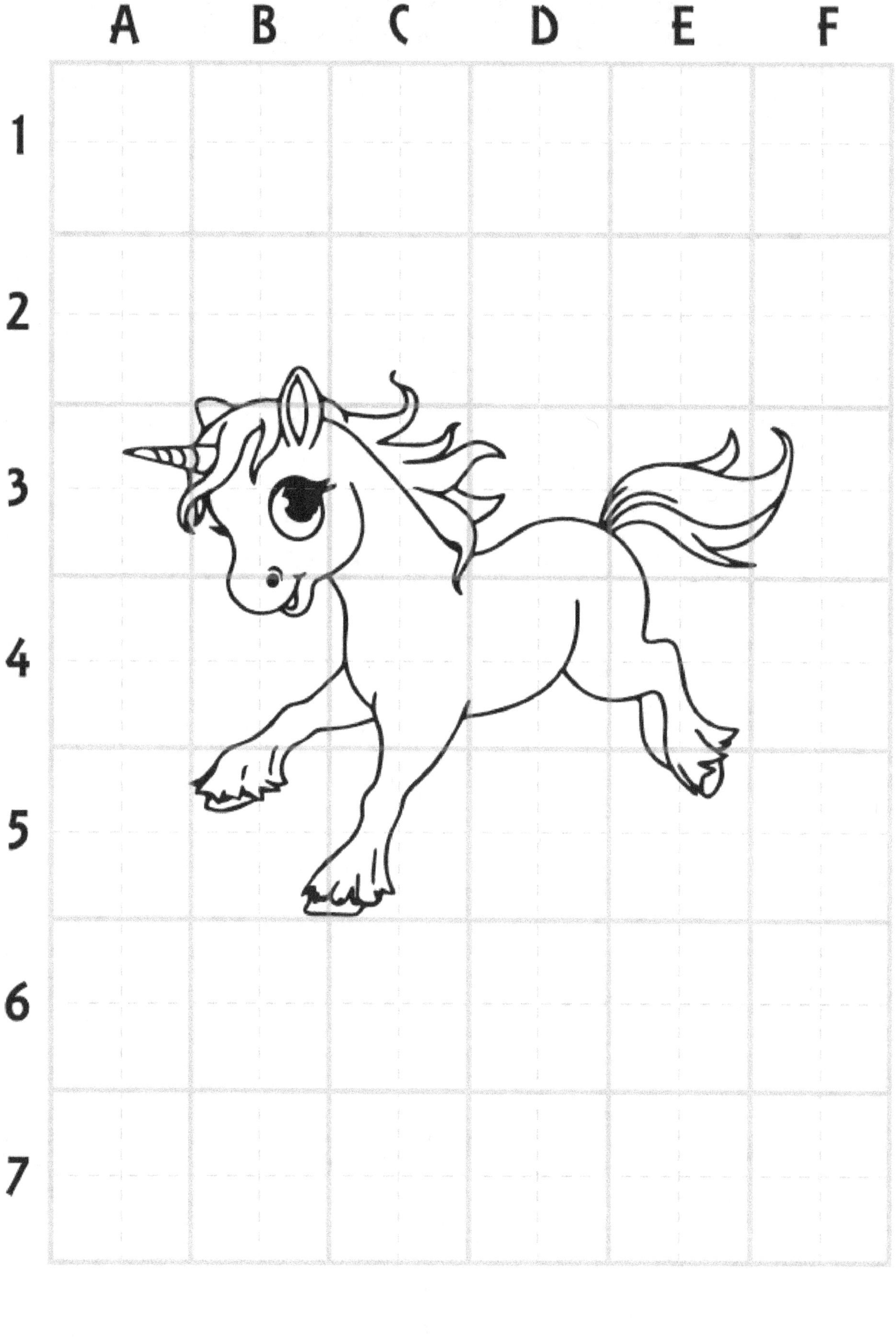
A
B
C
D
E
F
1
2
3
4
5
6
7

YOUR TURN!

	A	B	C	D	E	F
1						
2						
3						
4						
5						
6						
7						

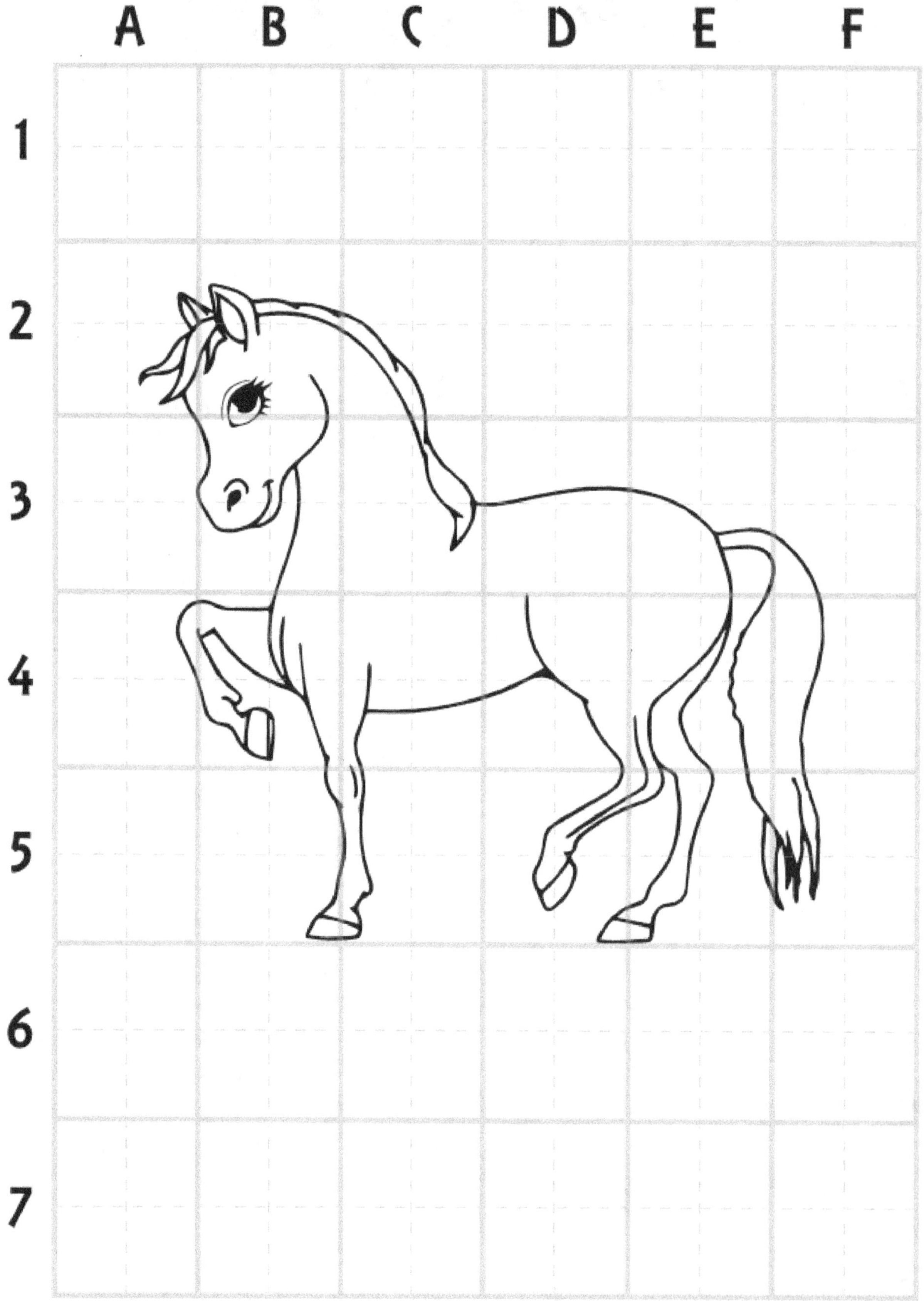
A
B
C
D
E
F
1
2
3
4
5
6
7

YOUR TURN!

	A	B	C	D	E	F
1						
2						
3						
4						
5						
6						
7						

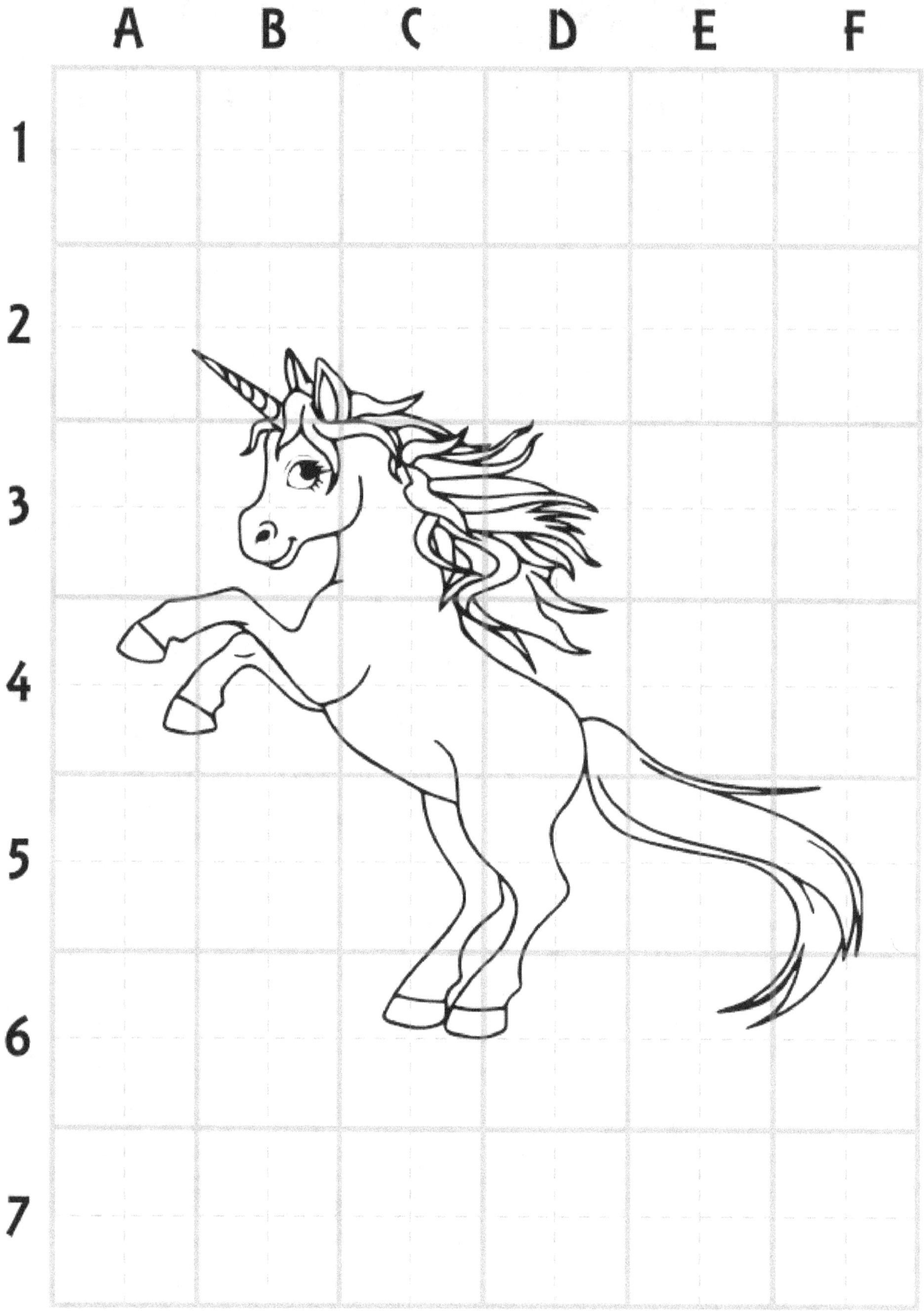
A
B
C
D
E
F
1
2
3
4
5
6
7

YOUR TURN!

	A	B	C	D	E	F
1						
2						
3						
4						
5						
6						
7						

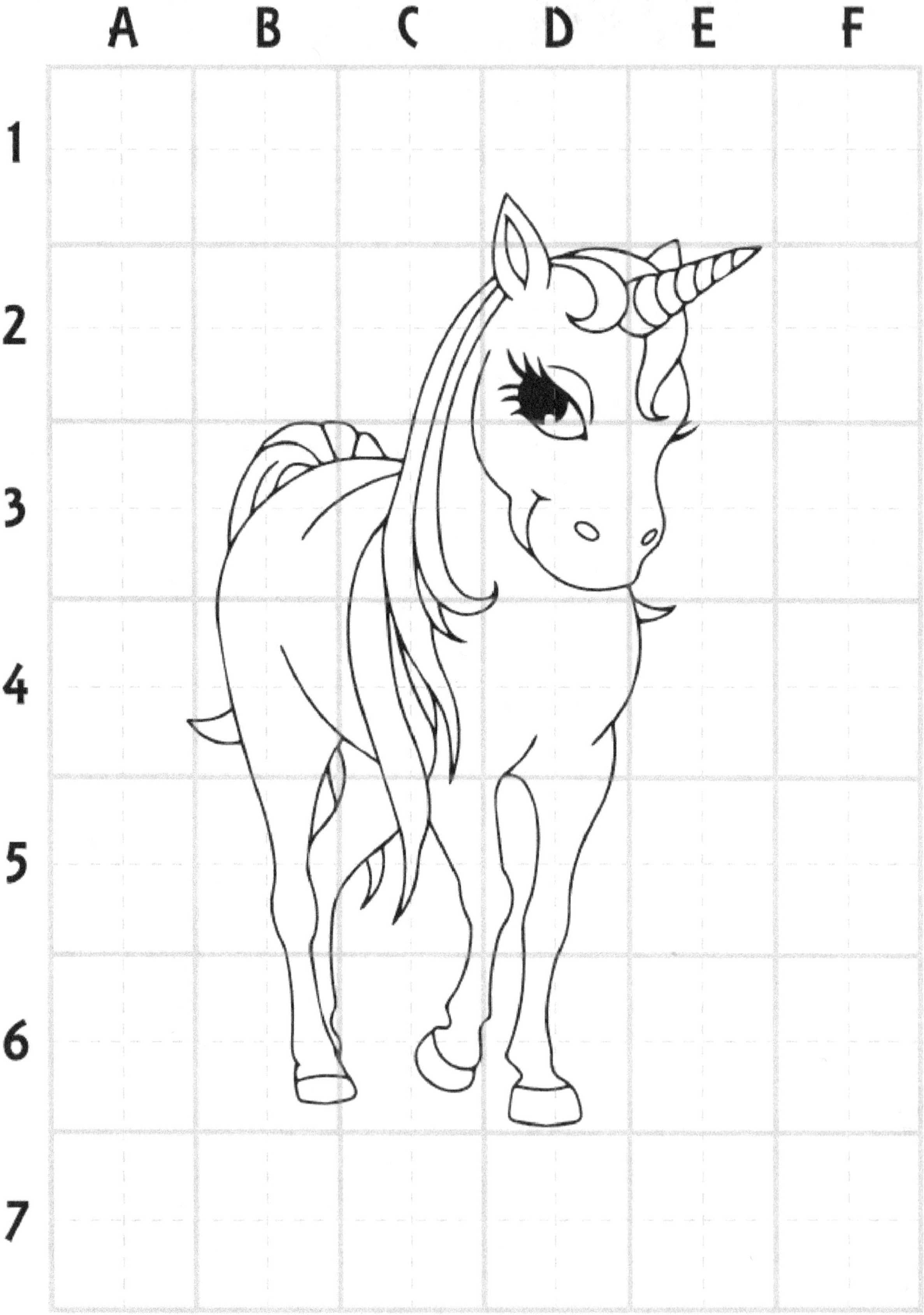
A
B
C
D
E
F
1
2
3
4
5
6
7

YOUR TURN!

	A	B	C	D	E	F
1						
2						
3						
4						
5						
6						
7						

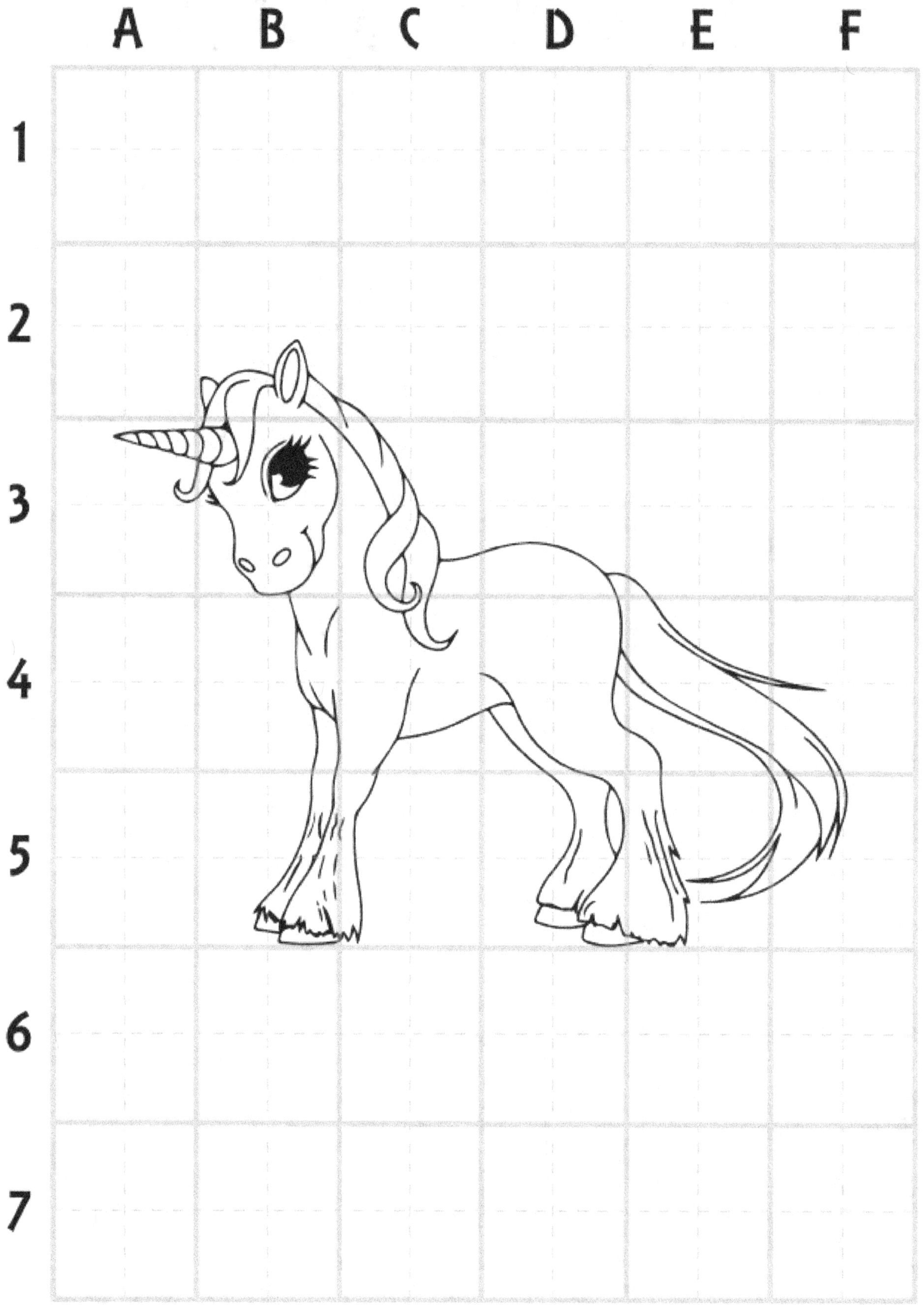
A B C D E F
1 2 3 4 5 6 7

YOUR TURN!

	A	B	C	D	E	F
1						
2						
3						
4						
5						
6						
7						

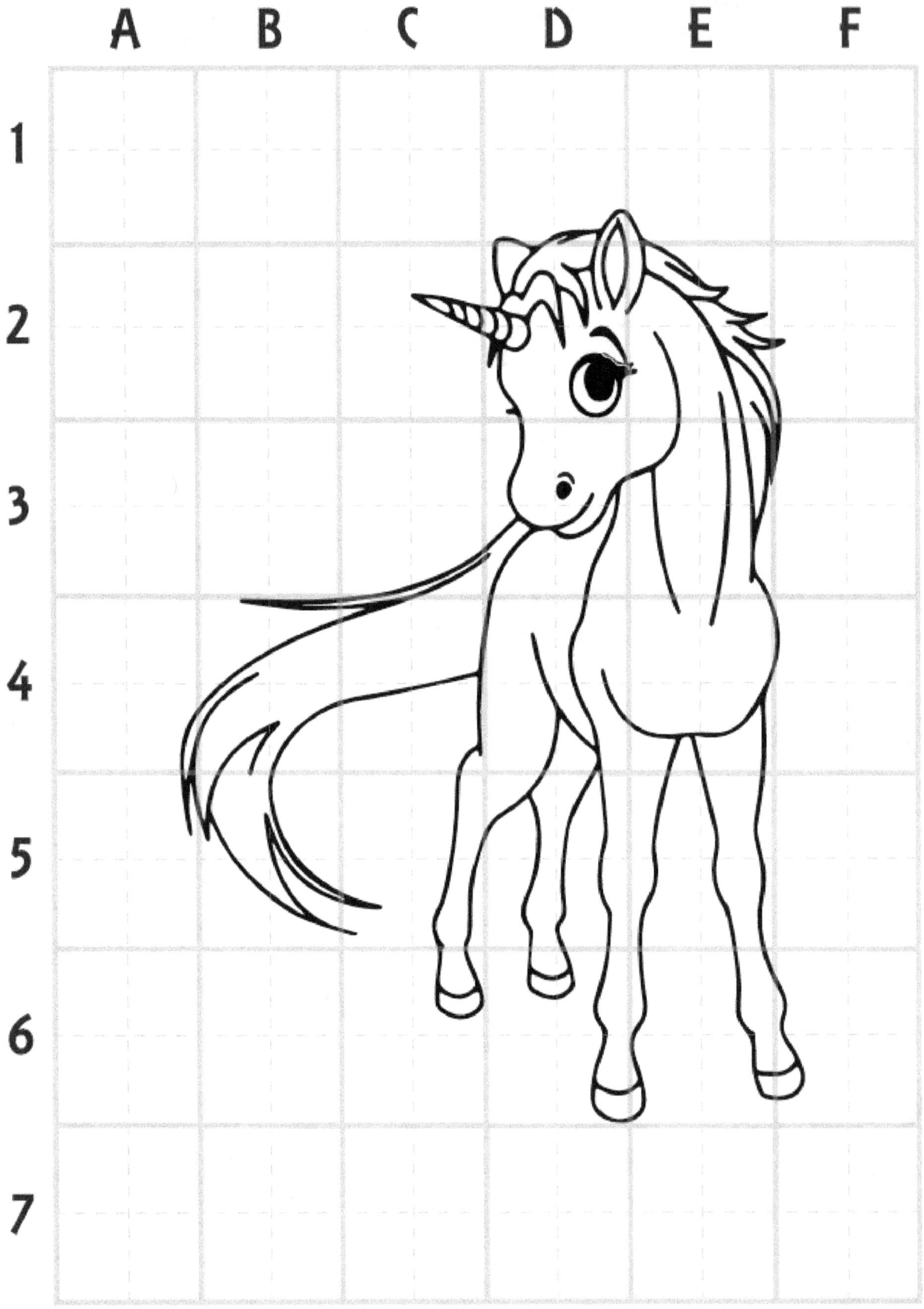

YOUR TURN!

	A	B	C	D	E	F
1						
2						
3						
4						
5						
6						
7						

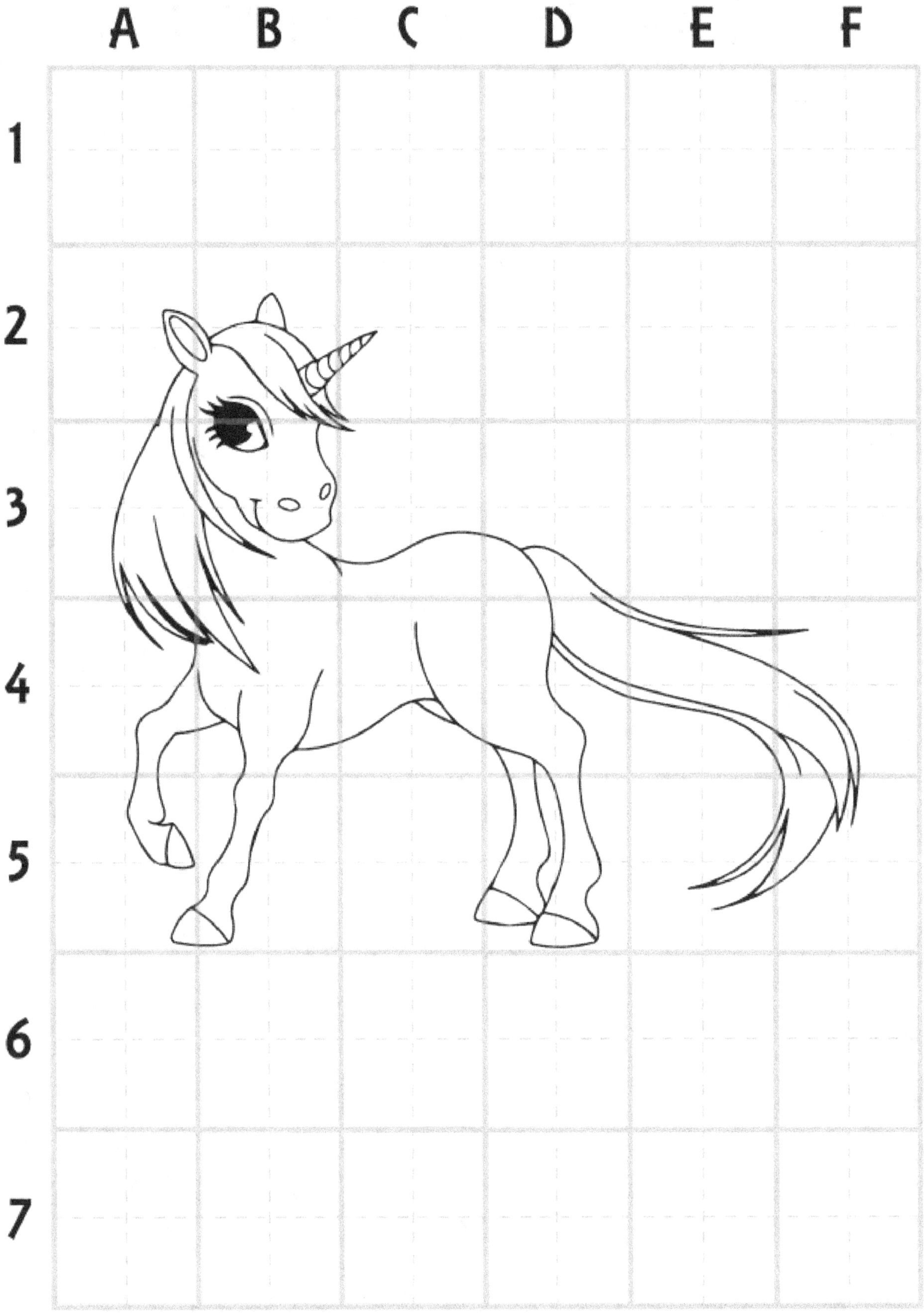
A
B
C
D
E
F
1
2
3
4
5
6
7

YOUR TURN!

	A	B	C	D	E	F
1						
2						
3						
4						
5						
6						
7						

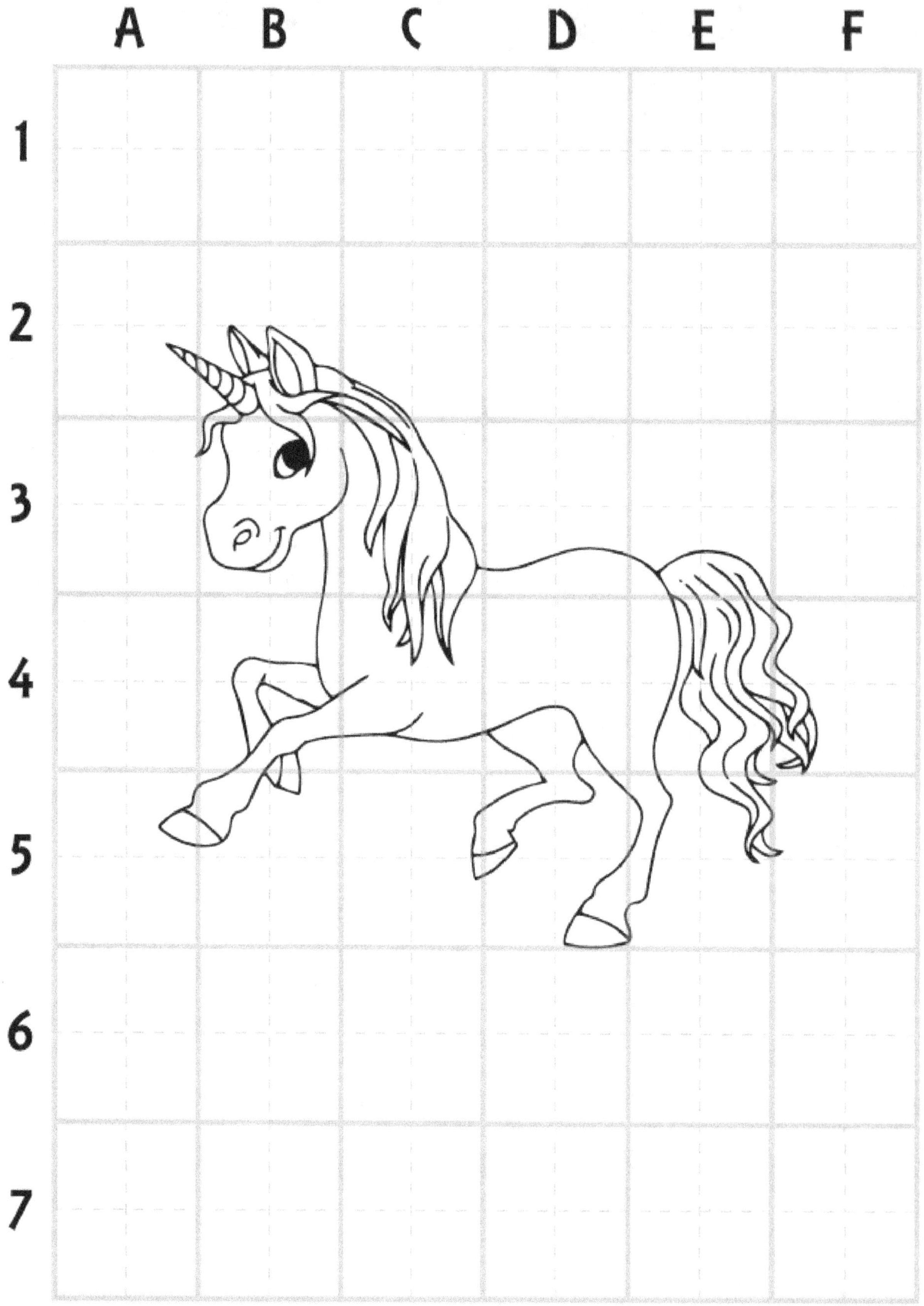
A
B
C
D
E
F
1
2
3
4
5
6
7

YOUR TURN!

	A	B	C	D	E	F
1						
2						
3						
4						
5						
6						
7						

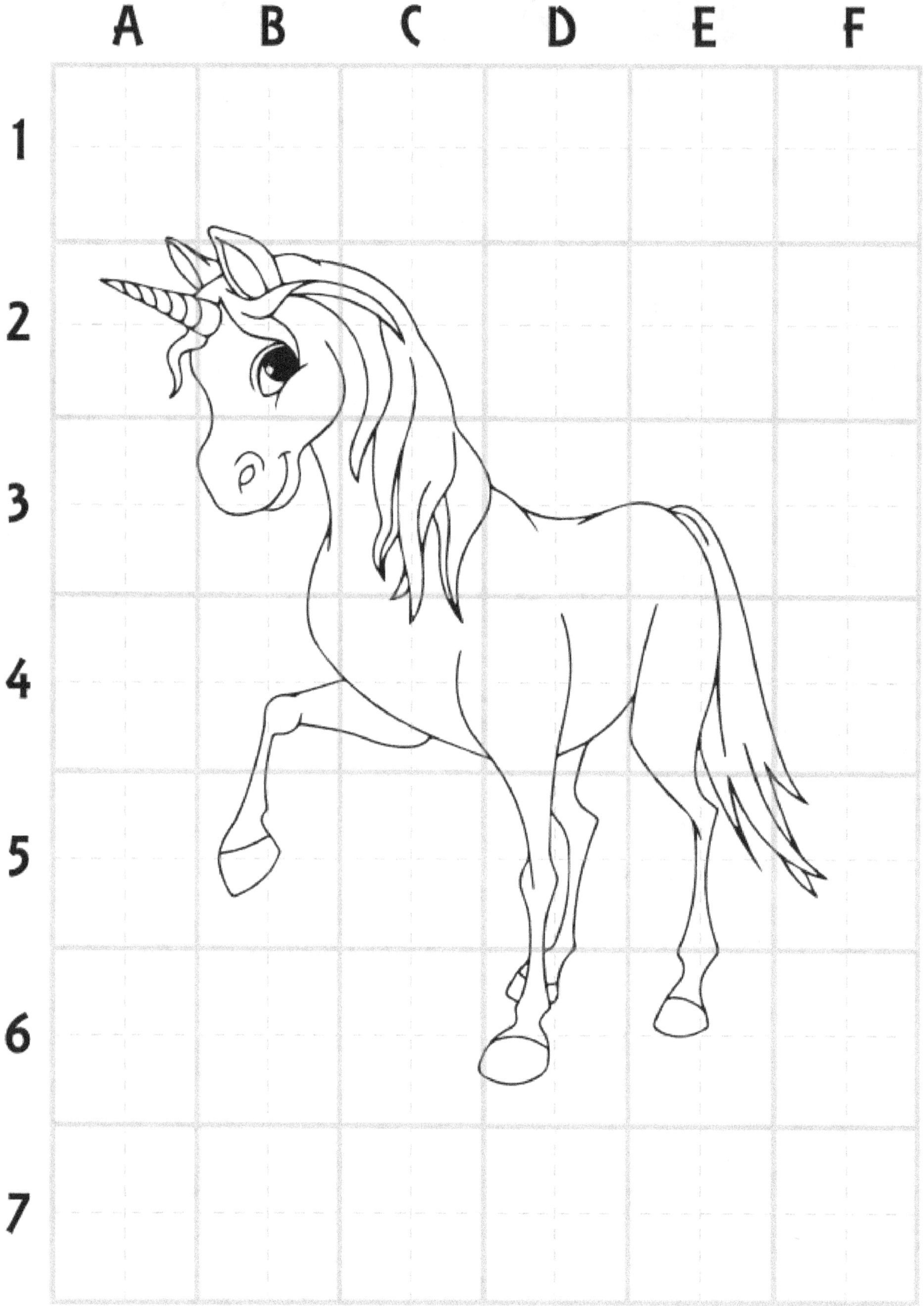
A B C D E F
1
2
3
4
5
6
7

YOUR TURN!

	A	B	C	D	E	F
1						
2						
3						
4						
5						
6						
7						

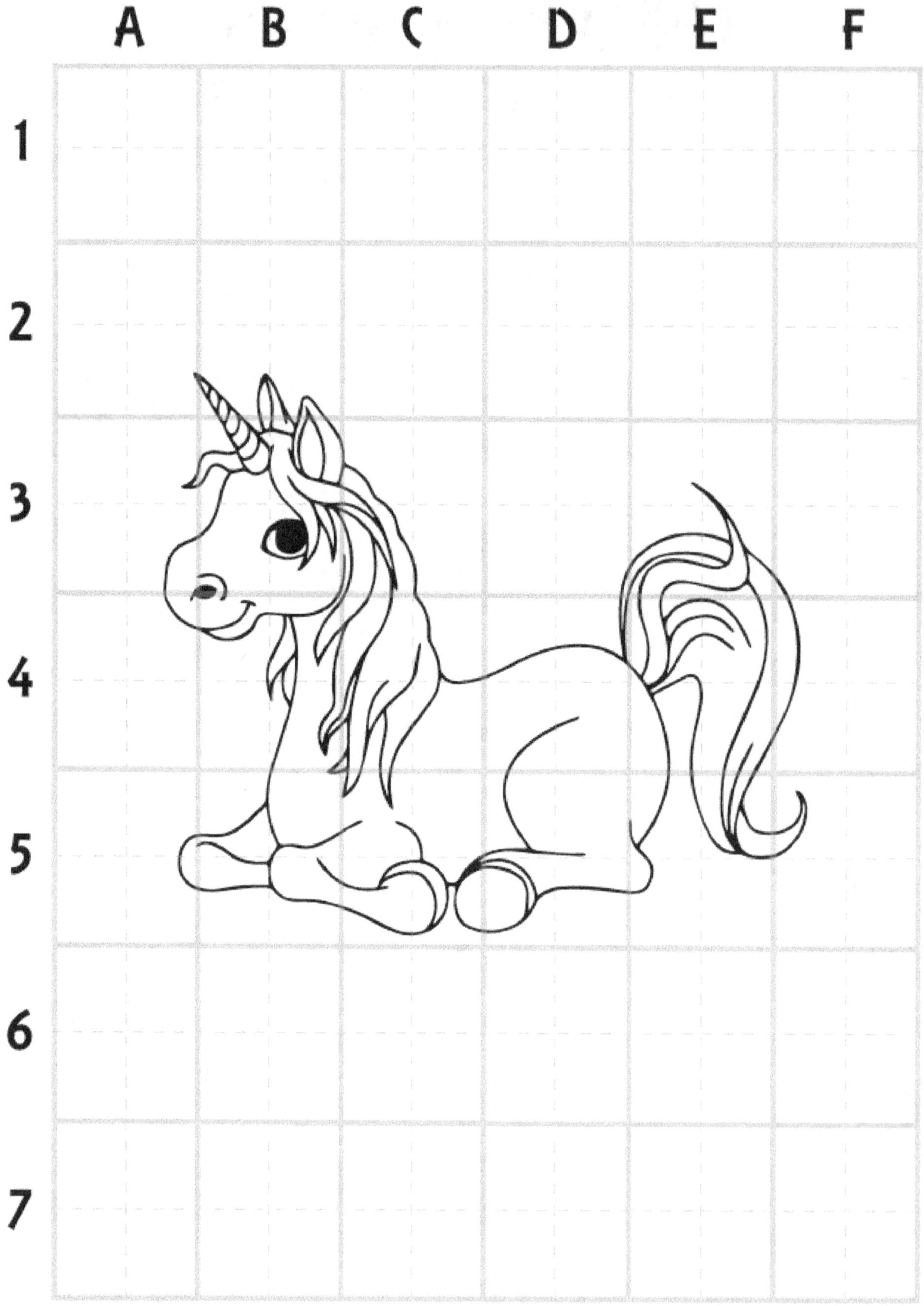
A
B
C
D
E
F
1
2
3
4
5
6
7

YOUR TURN!

	A	B	C	D	E	F
1						
2						
3						
4						
5						
6						
7						

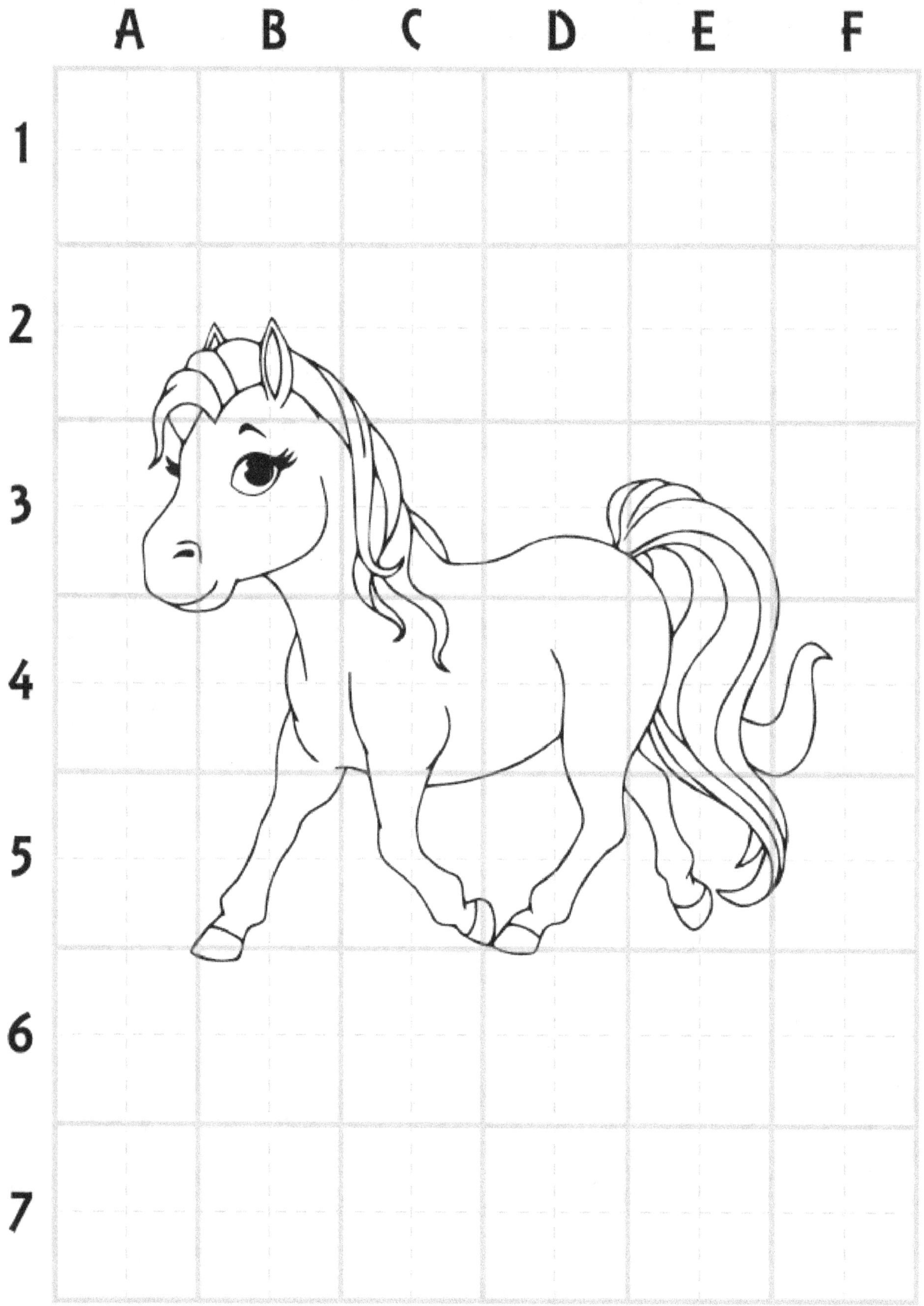
A B C D E F
1
2
3
4
5
6
7

YOUR TURN!

	A	B	C	D	E	F
1						
2						
3						
4						
5						
6						
7						

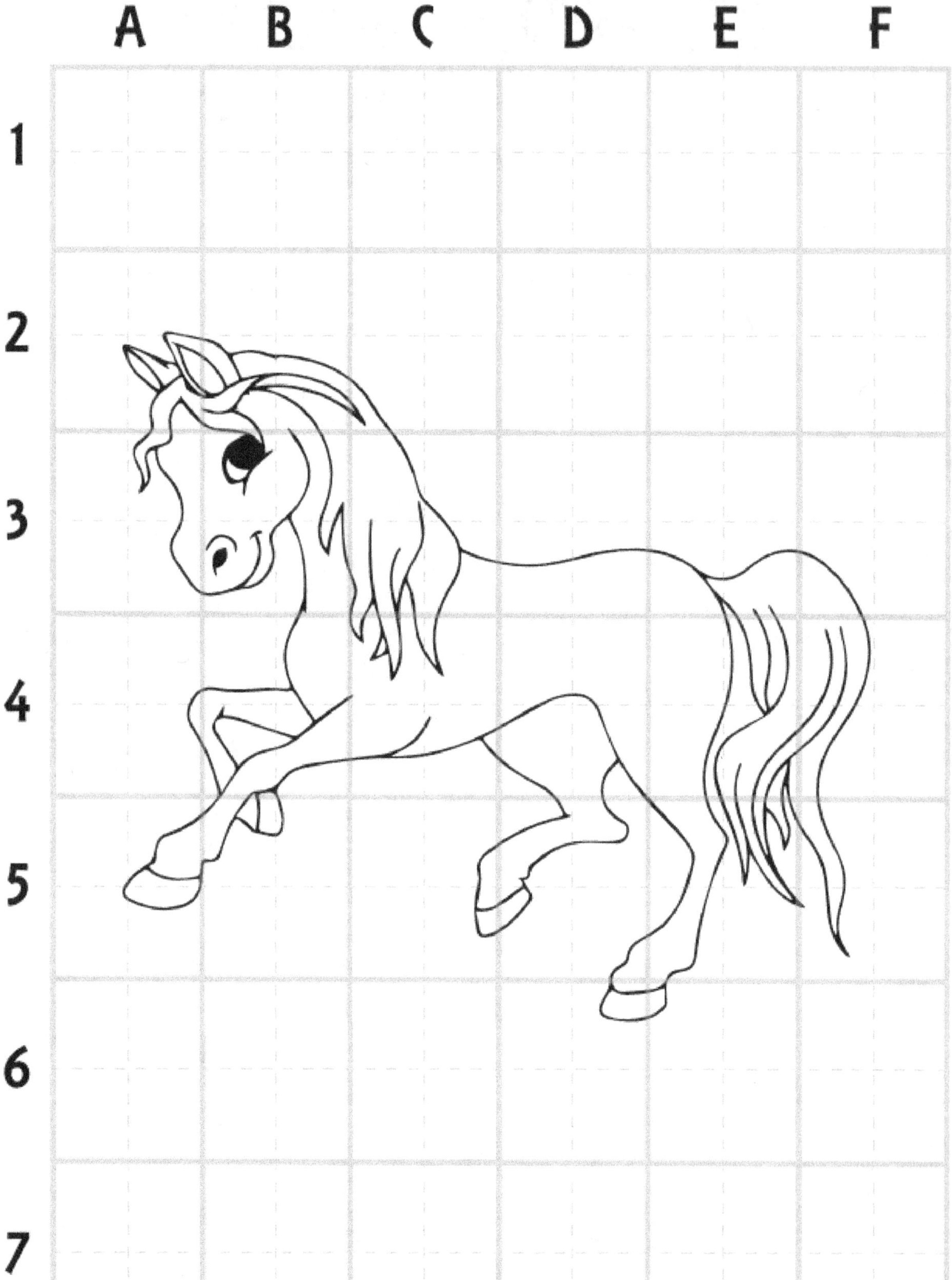
A B C D E F
1 2 3 4 5 6 7

YOUR TURN!

	A	B	C	D	E	F
1						
2						
3						
4						
5						
6						
7						

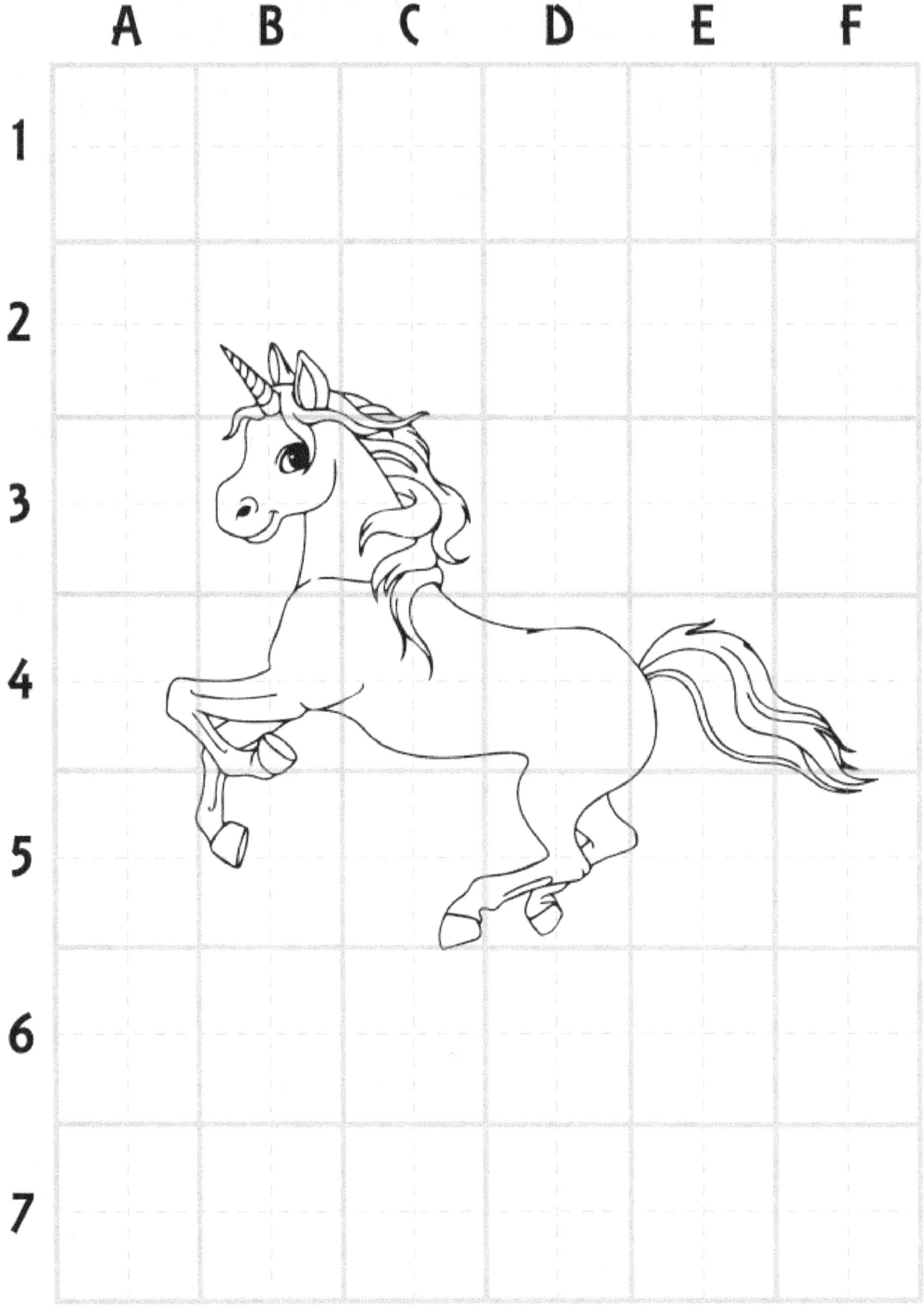
A
B
C
D
E
F
1
2
3
4
5
6
7

YOUR TURN!

	A	B	C	D	E	F
1						
2						
3						
4						
5						
6						
7						

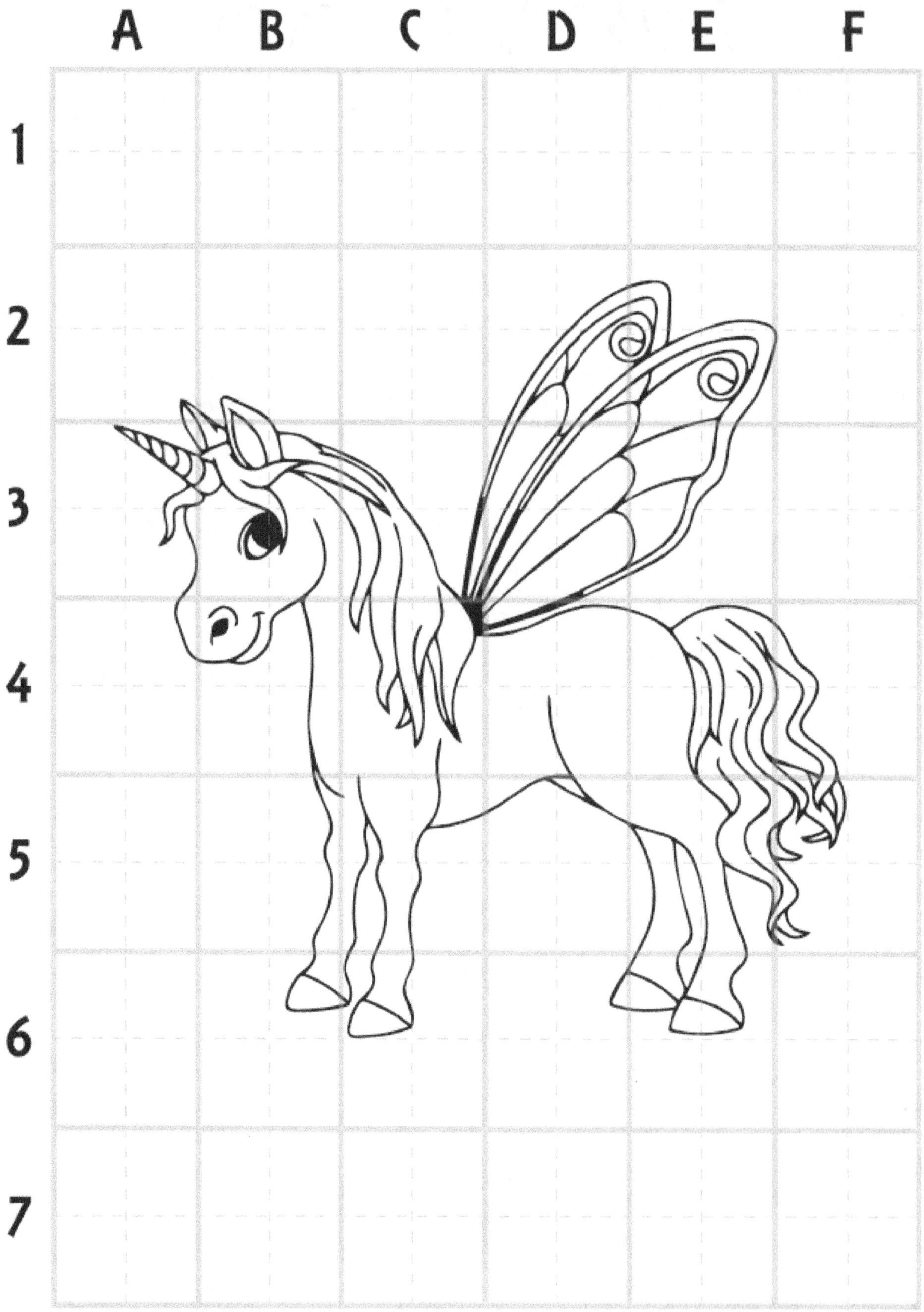
A
B
C
D
E
F
1
2
3
4
5
6
7

YOUR TURN!

	A	B	C	D	E	F
1						
2						
3						
4						
5						
6						
7						

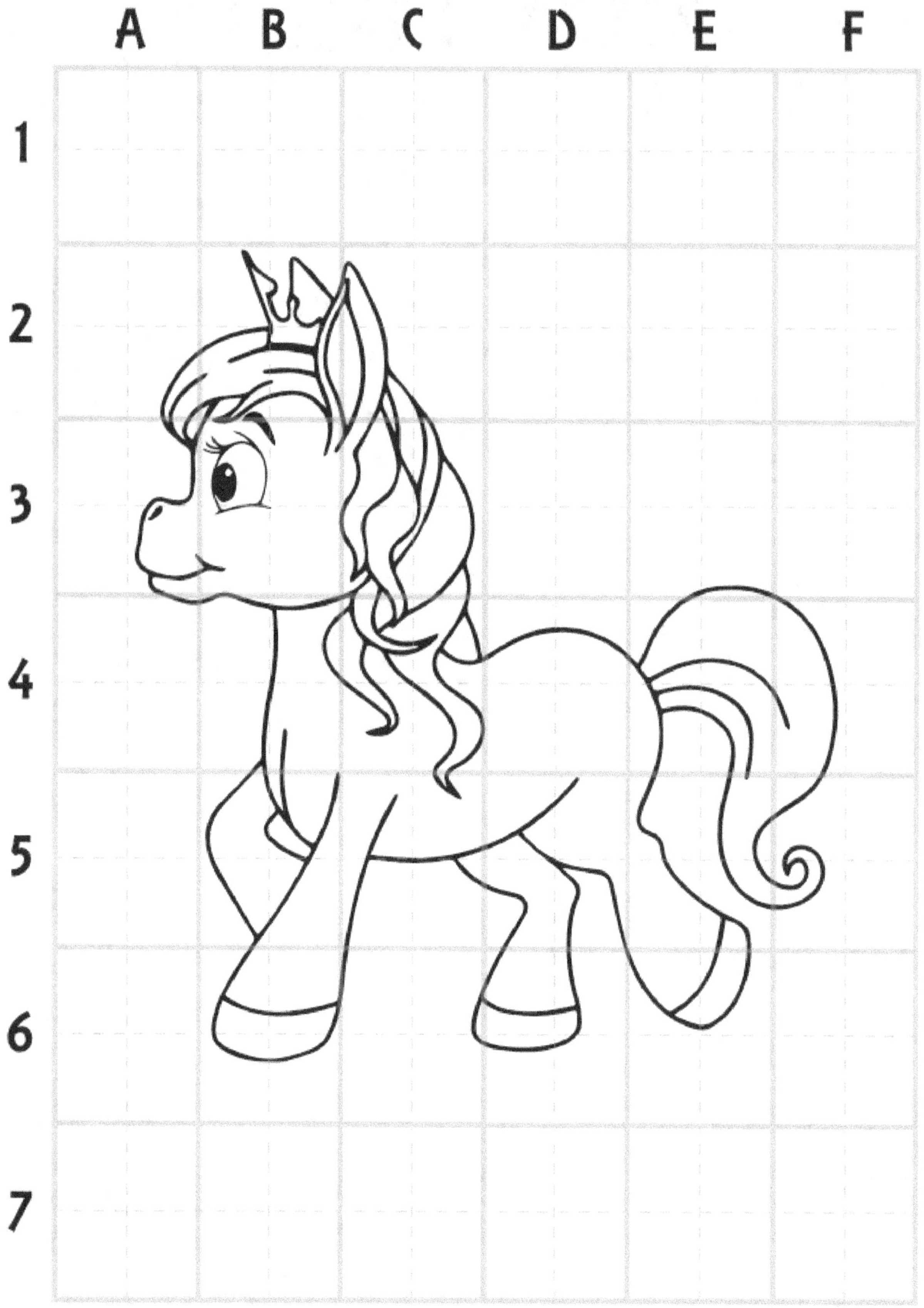
A
B
C
D
E
F
1
2
3
4
5
6
7

YOUR TURN!

	A	B	C	D	E	F
1						
2						
3						
4						
5						
6						
7						

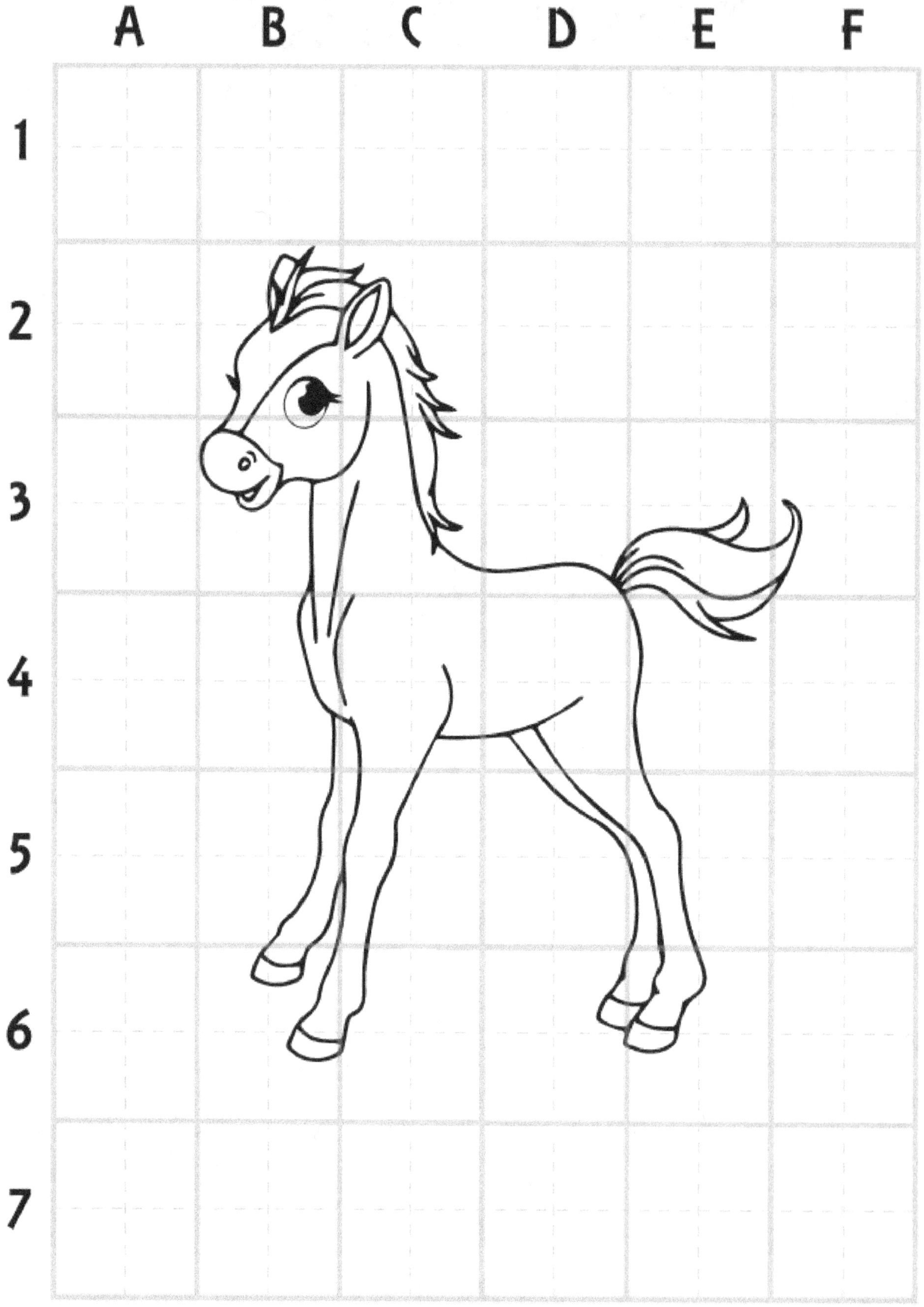
A B C D E F
1
2
3
4
5
6
7

YOUR TURN!

	A	B	C	D	E	F
1						
2						
3						
4						
5						
6						
7						

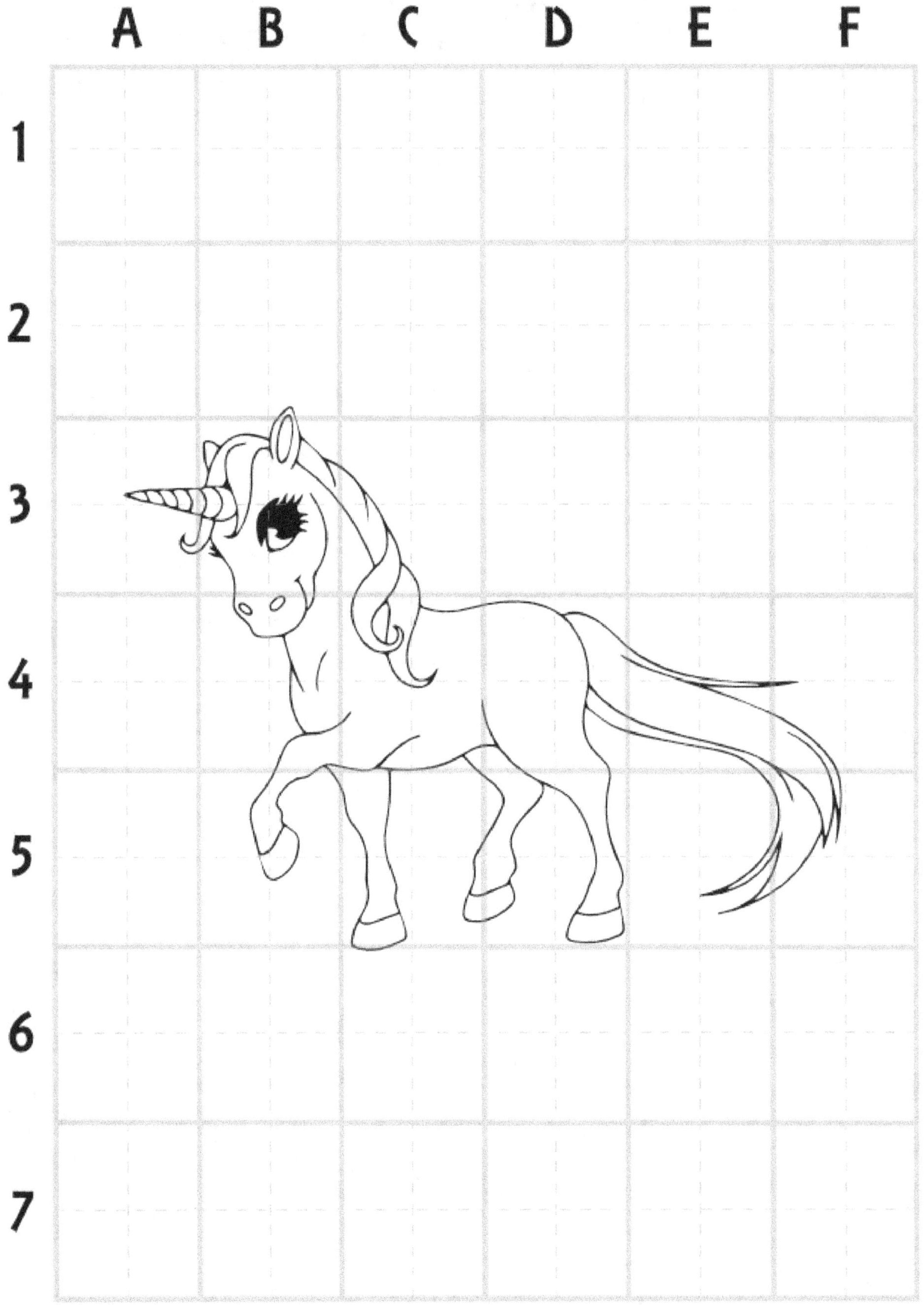
A
B
C
D
E
F
1
2
3
4
5
6
7

YOUR TURN!

	A	B	C	D	E	F
1						
2						
3						
4						
5						
6						
7						

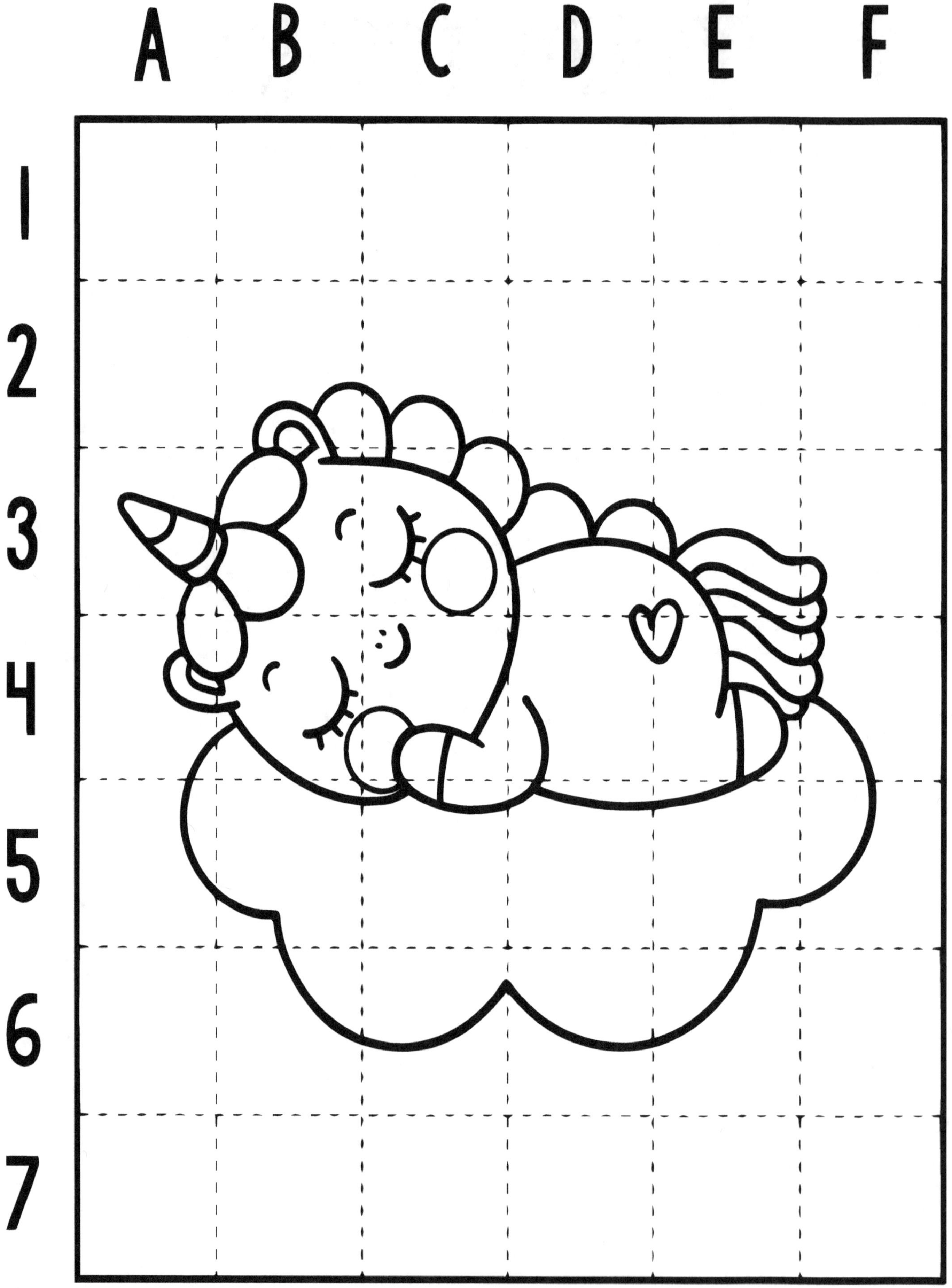
A B C D E F
1
2
3
4
5
6
7

YOUR TURN!

	A	B	C	D	E	F
1						
2						
3						
4						
5						
6						
7						

A B C D E F

1
2
3
4
5
6
7

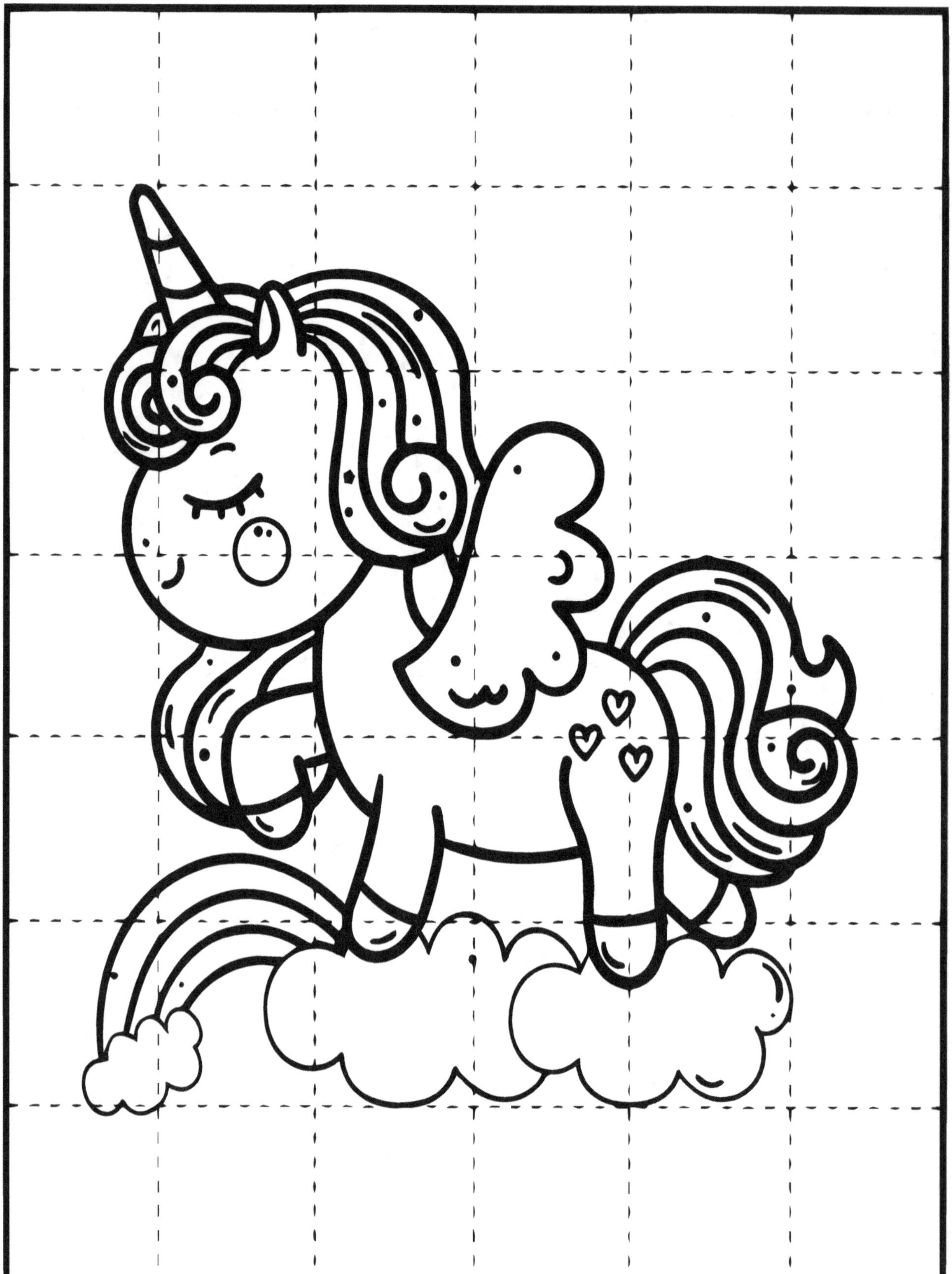

YOUR TURN!

	A	B	C	D	E	F
1						
2						
3						
4						
5						
6						
7						

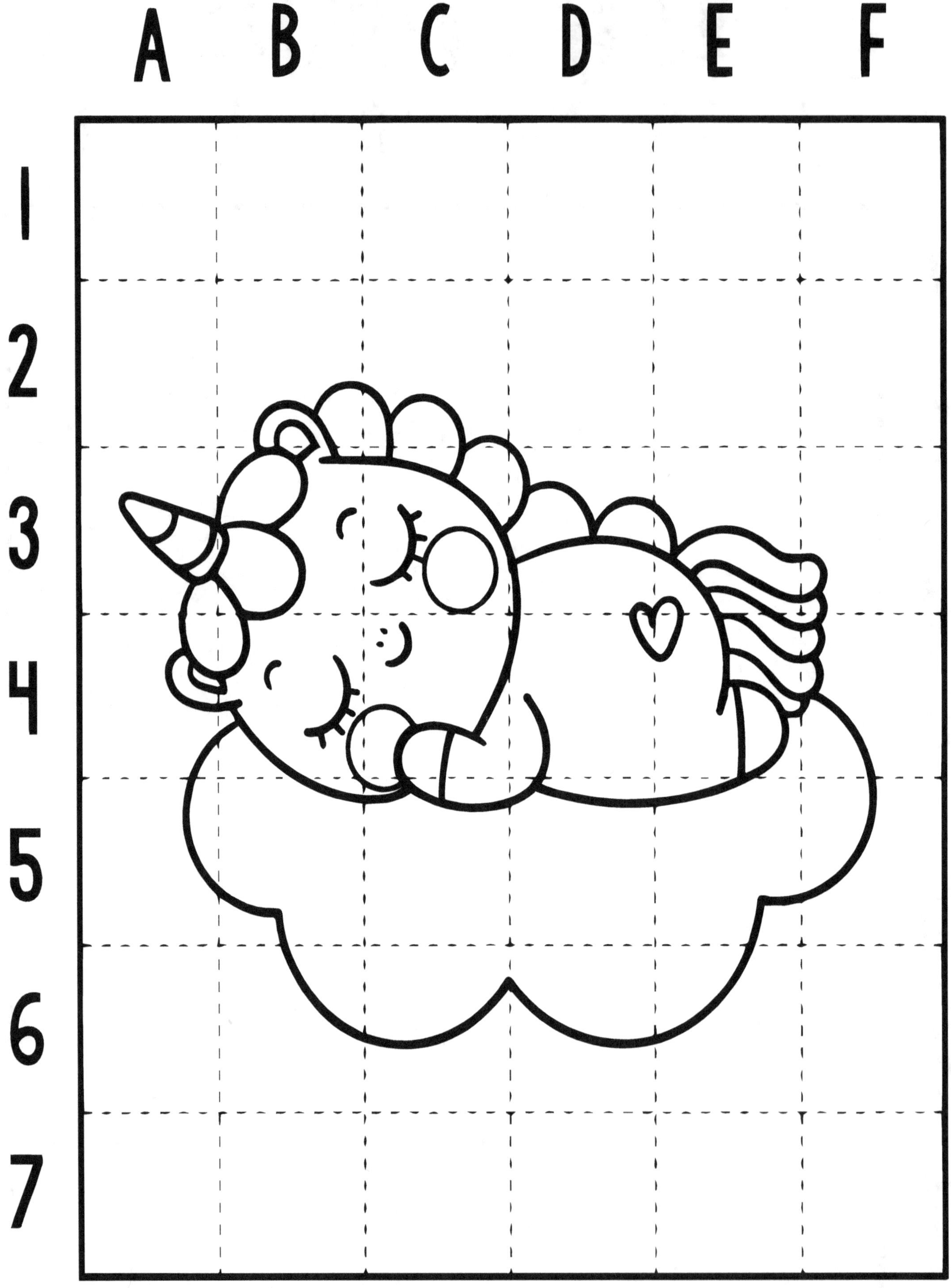
A B C D E F
1
2
3
4
5
6
7

YOUR TURN!

	A	B	C	D	E	F
1						
2						
3						
4						
5						
6						
7						

A B C D E F

1
2
3
4
5
6
7

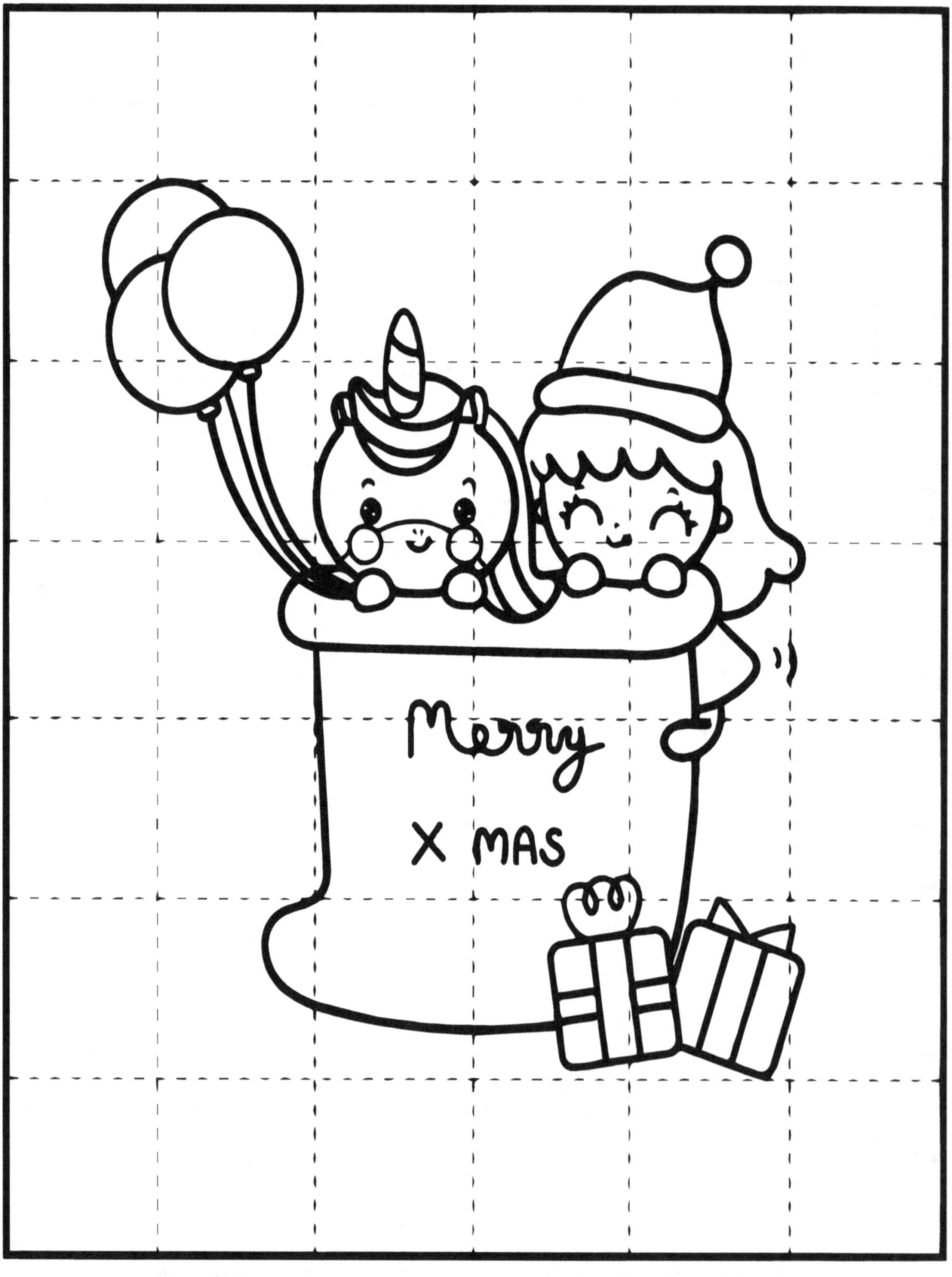

YOUR TURN!

	A	B	C	D	E	F
1						
2						
3						
4						
5						
6						
7						

A B C D E F

1
2
3
4
5
6
7

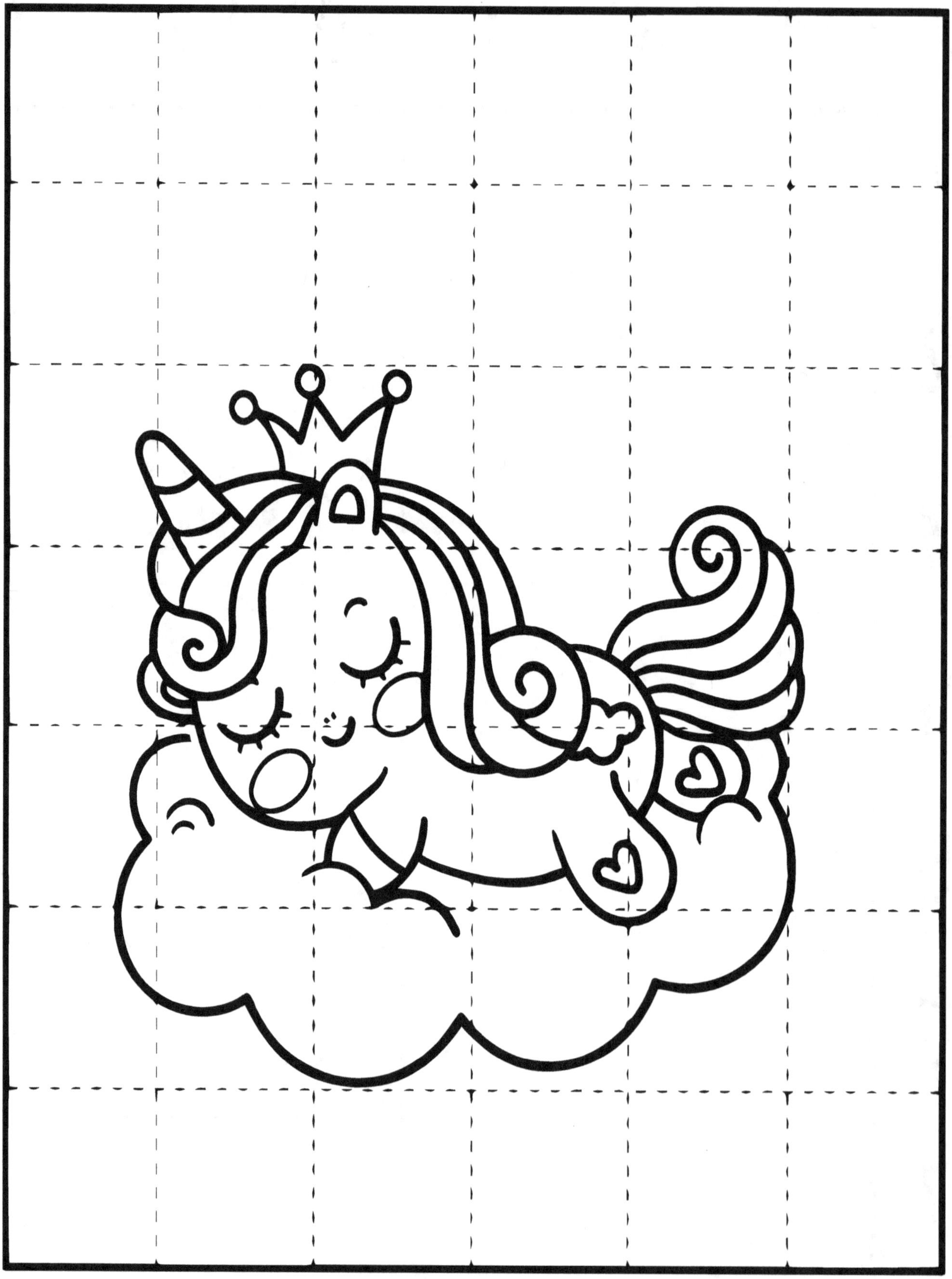

YOUR TURN!

	A	B	C	D	E	F
1						
2						
3						
4						
5						
6						
7						

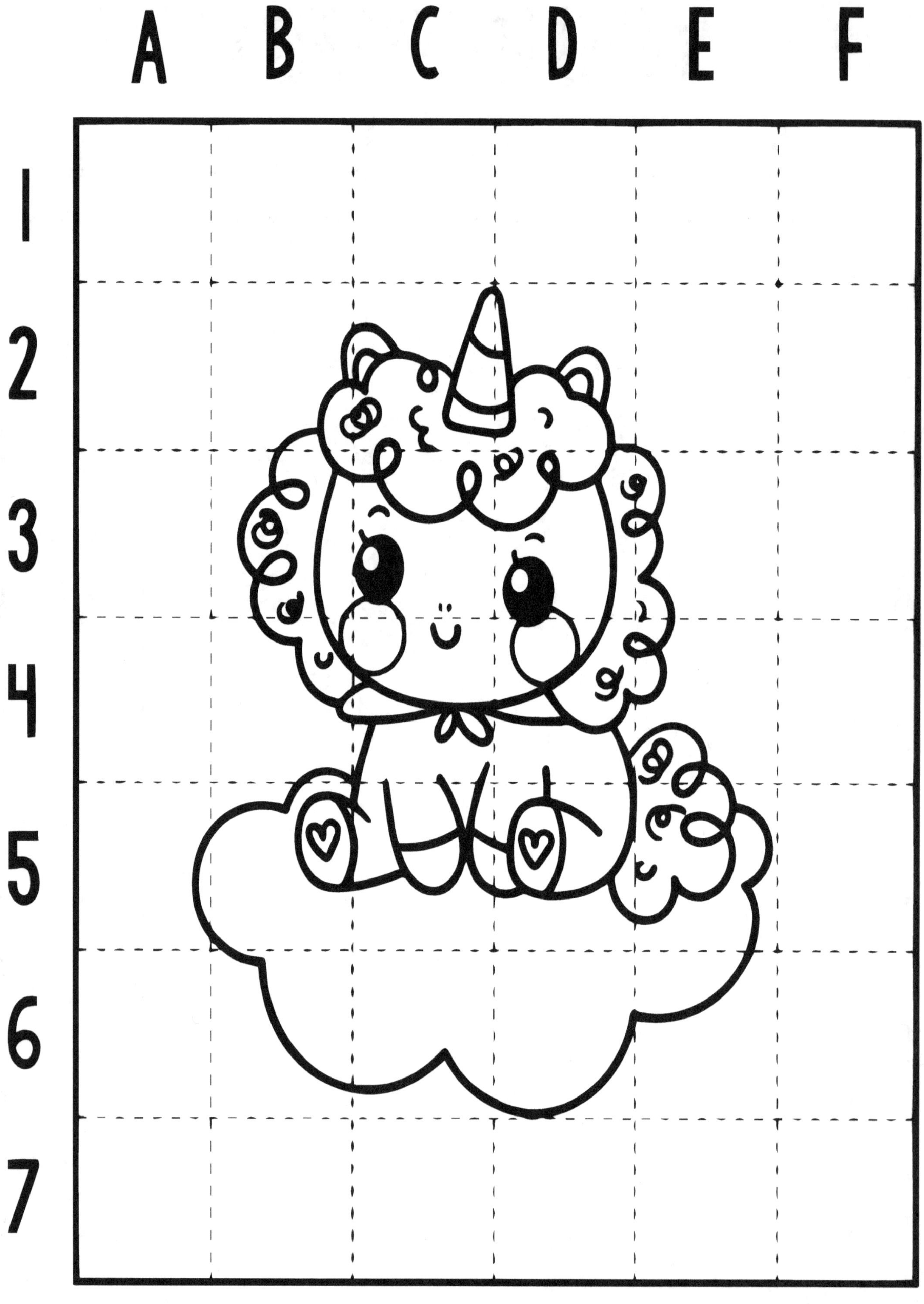
A B C D E F
1
2
3
4
5
6
7

YOUR TURN!

	A	B	C	D	E	F
1						
2						
3						
4						
5						
6						
7						

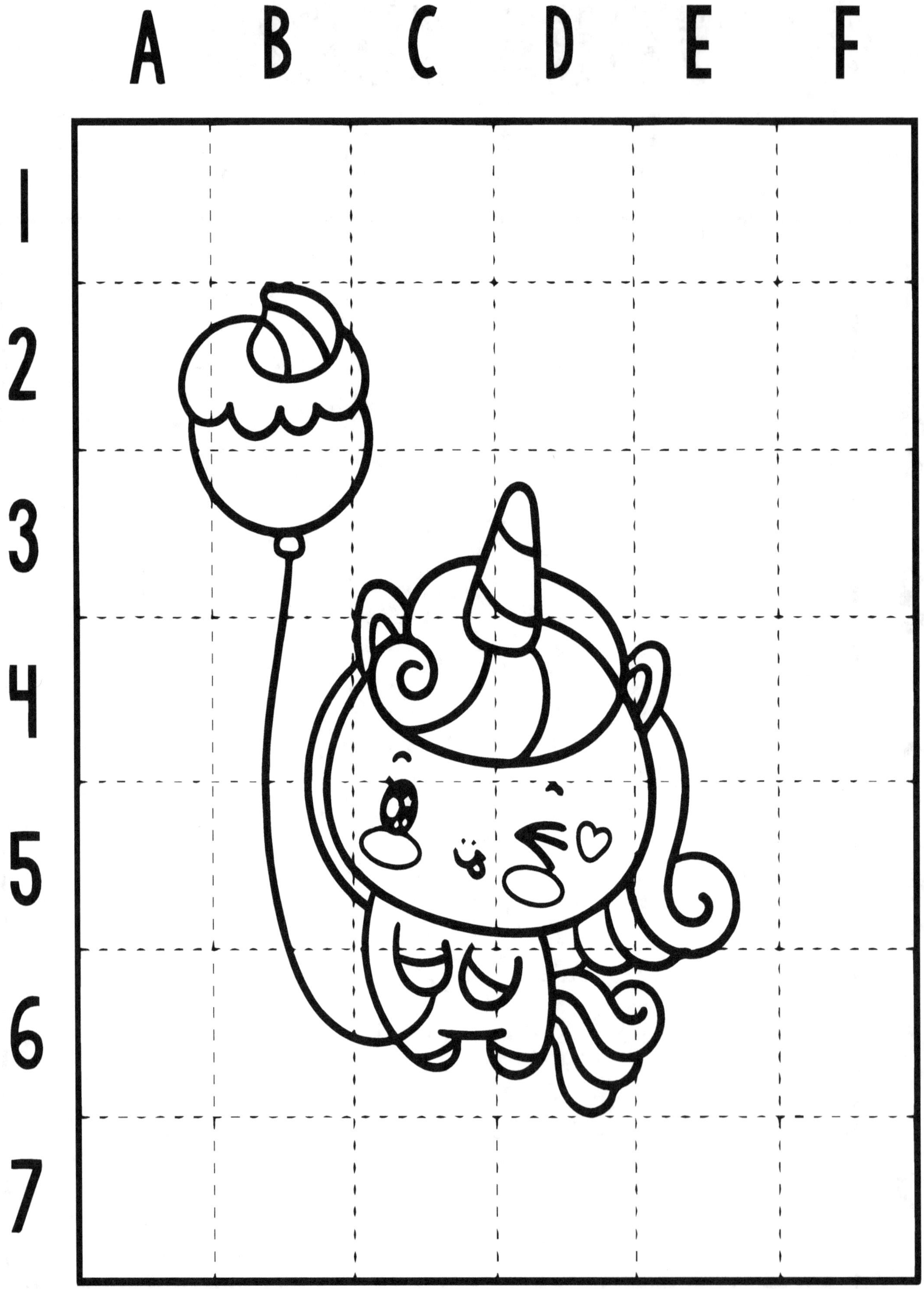
A B C D E F
1
2
3
4
5
6
7

YOUR TURN!

	A	B	C	D	E	F
1						
2						
3						
4						
5						
6						
7						

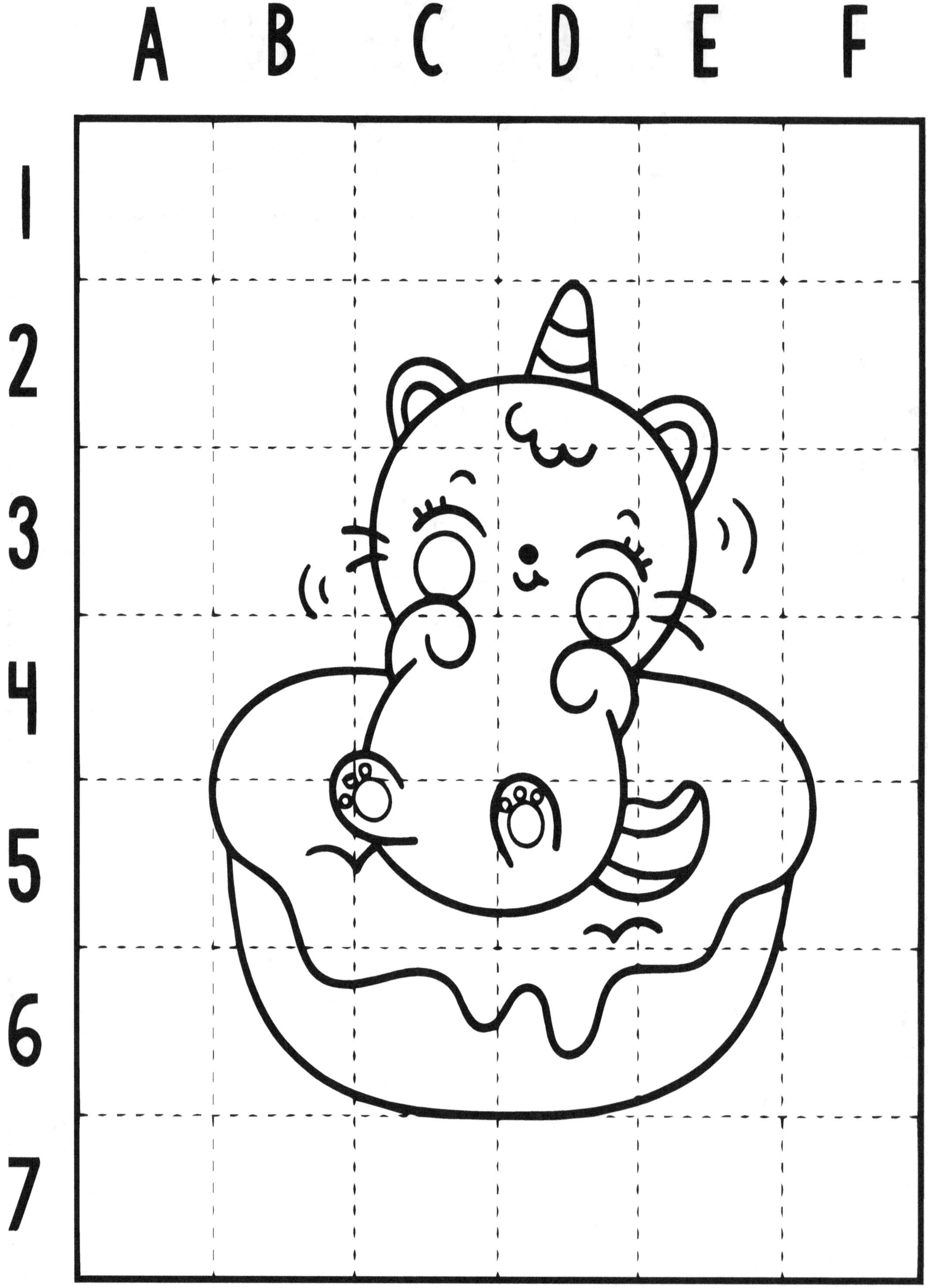
A B C D E F
1
2
3
4
5
6
7

YOUR TURN!

	A	B	C	D	E	F
1						
2						
3						
4						
5						
6						
7						

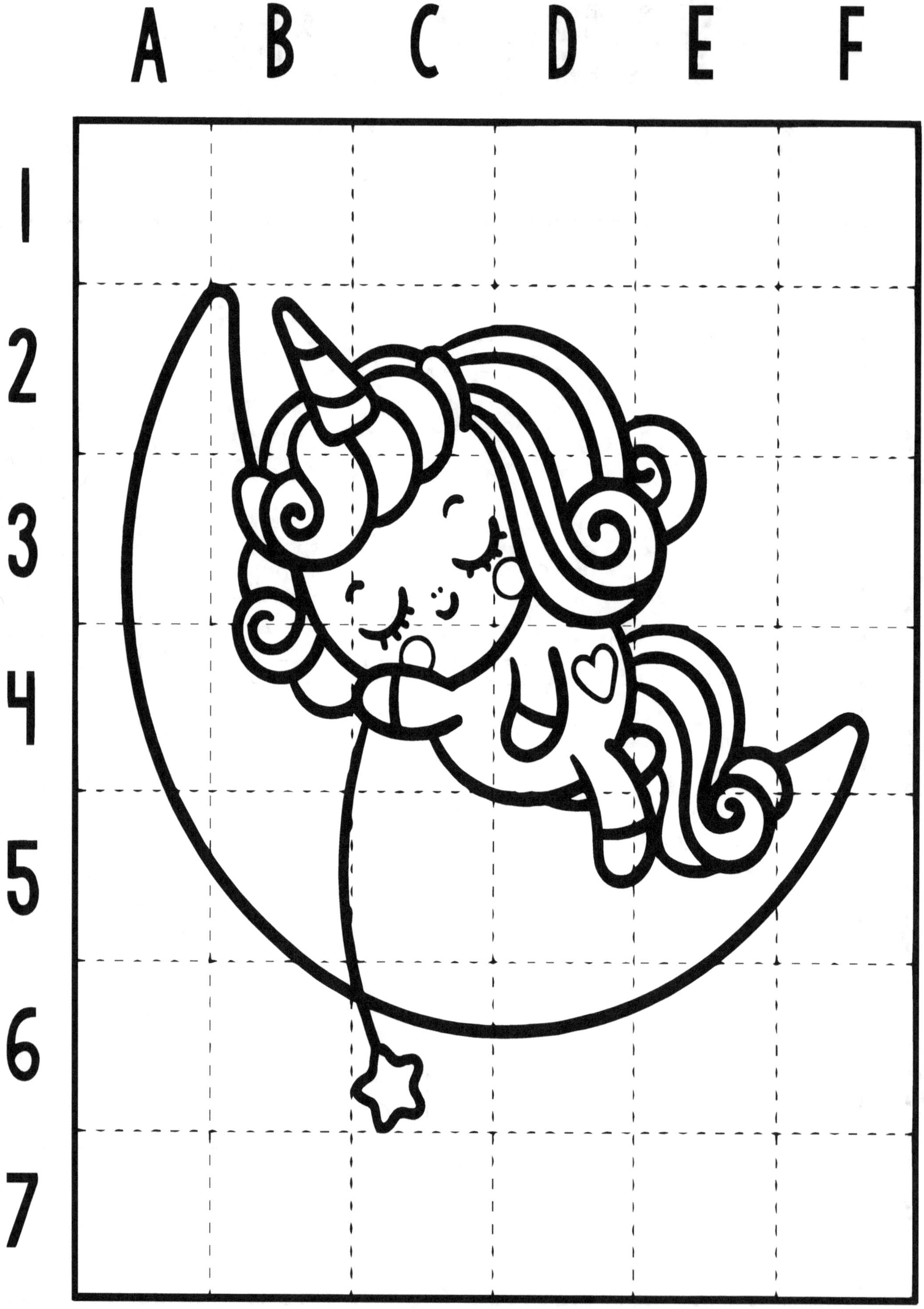
A B C D E F
1
2
3
4
5
6
7

YOUR TURN!

	A	B	C	D	E	F
1						
2						
3						
4						
5						
6						
7						

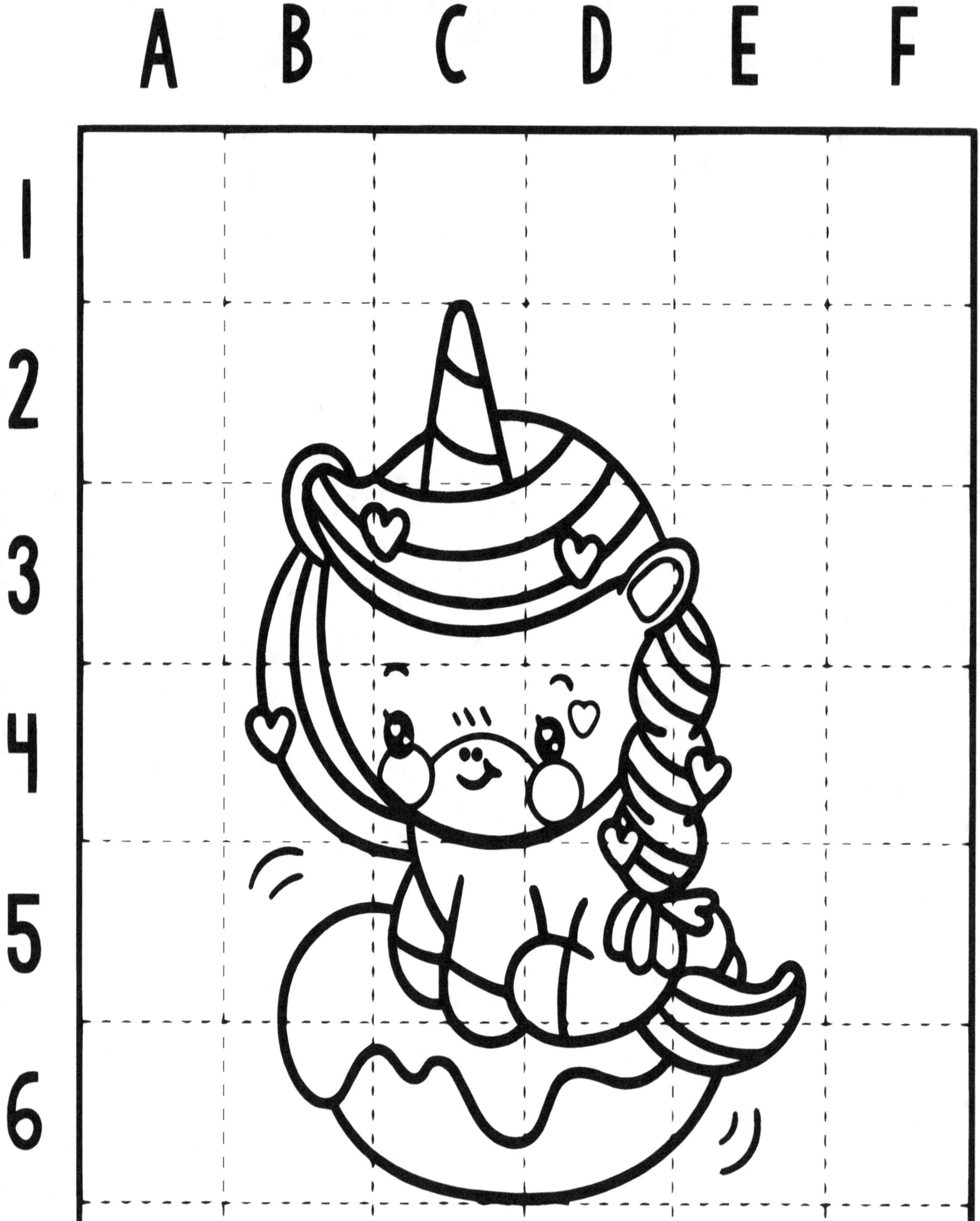
A B C D E F
1
2
3
4
5
6
7

YOUR TURN!

	A	B	C	D	E	F
1						
2						
3						
4						
5						
6						
7						

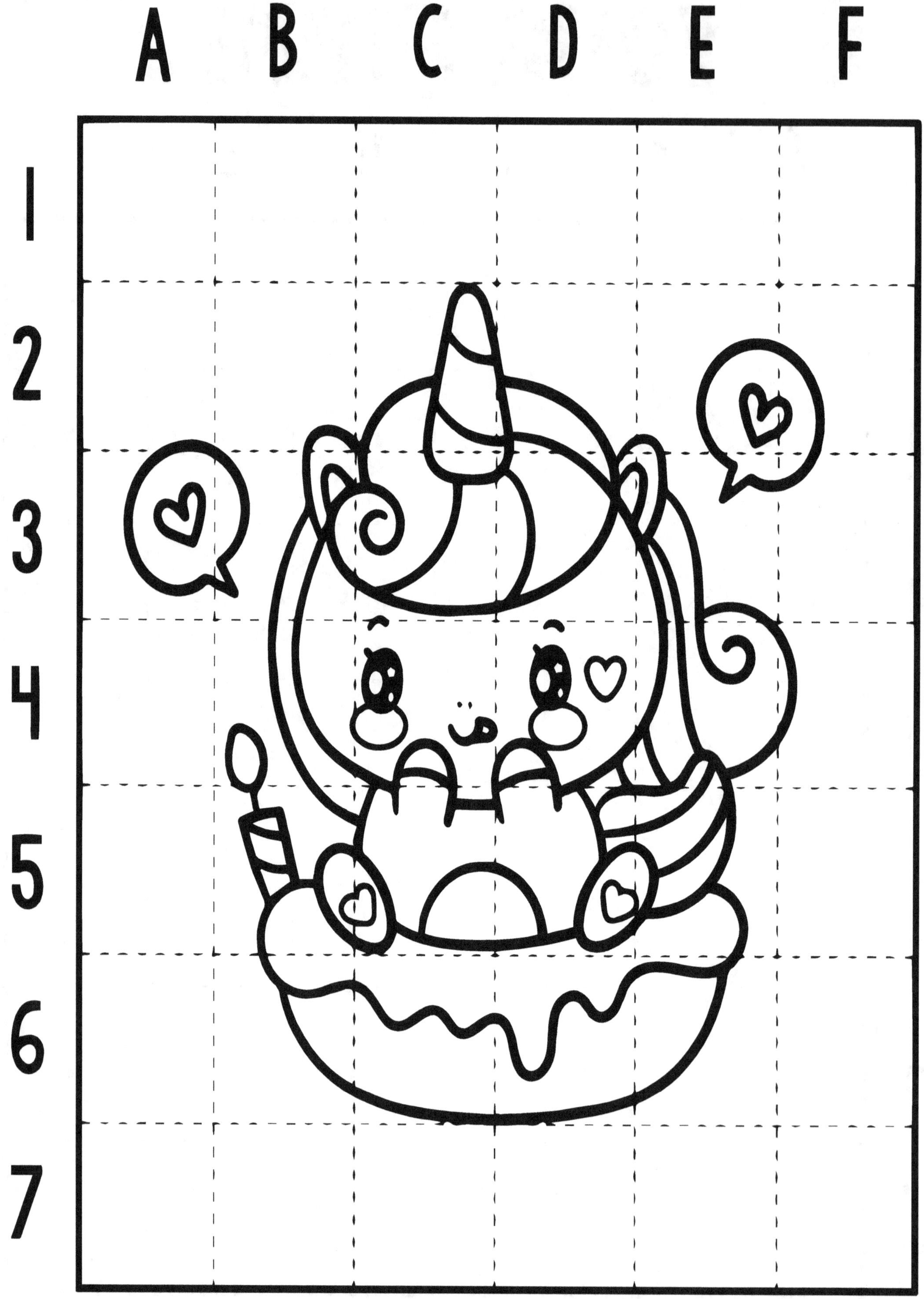
A B C D E F
1
2
3
4
5
6
7

YOUR TURN!

	A	B	C	D	E	F
1						
2						
3						
4						
5						
6						
7						

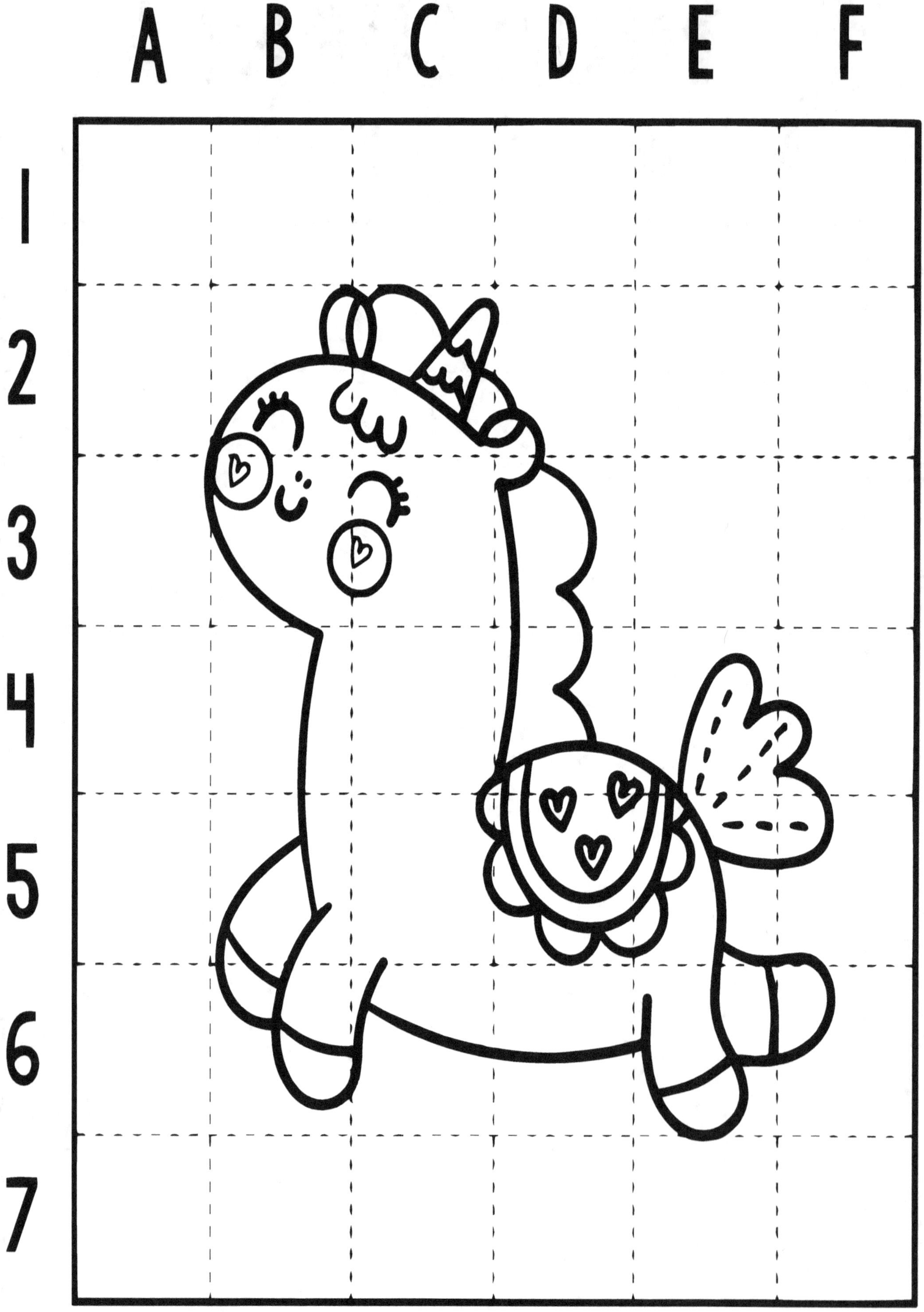
A B C D E F
1
2
3
4
5
6
7

YOUR TURN!

	A	B	C	D	E	F
1						
2						
3						
4						
5						
6						
7						

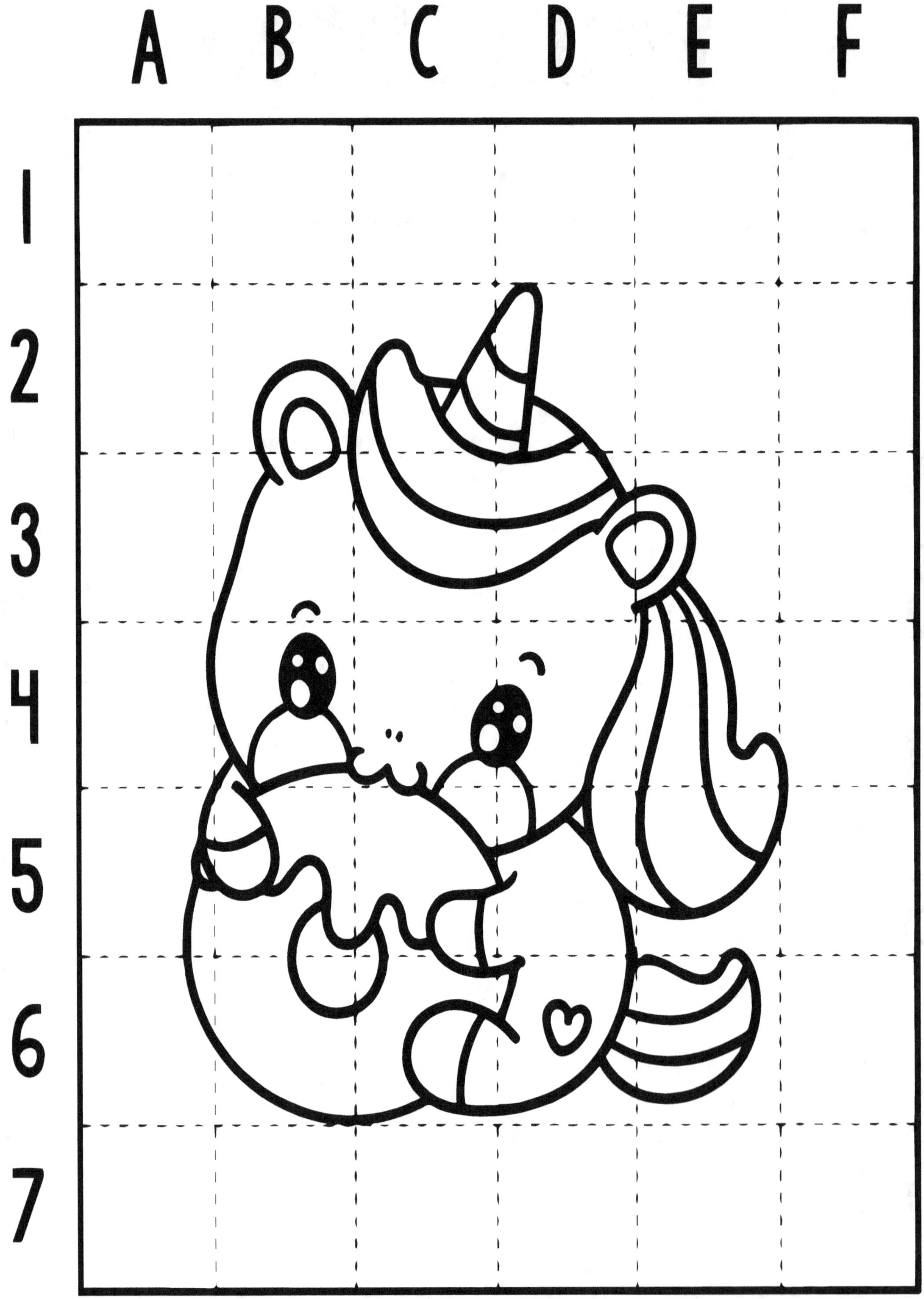
A B C D E F
1
2
3
4
5
6
7

YOUR TURN!

	A	B	C	D	E	F
1						
2						
3						
4						
5						
6						
7						

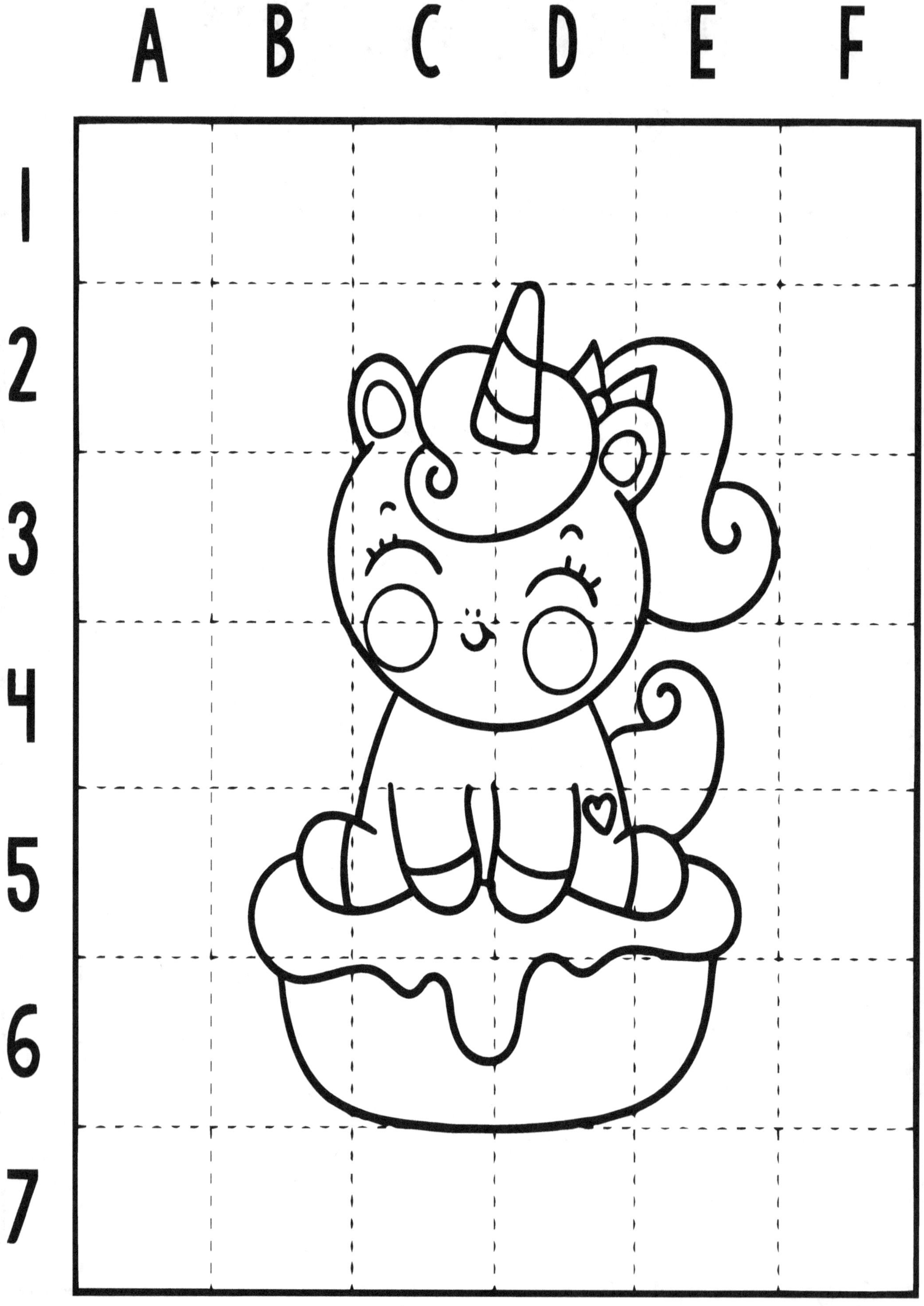
A
B
C
D
E
F
1
2
3
4
5
6
7

YOUR TURN!

	A	B	C	D	E	F
1						
2						
3						
4						
5						
6						
7						

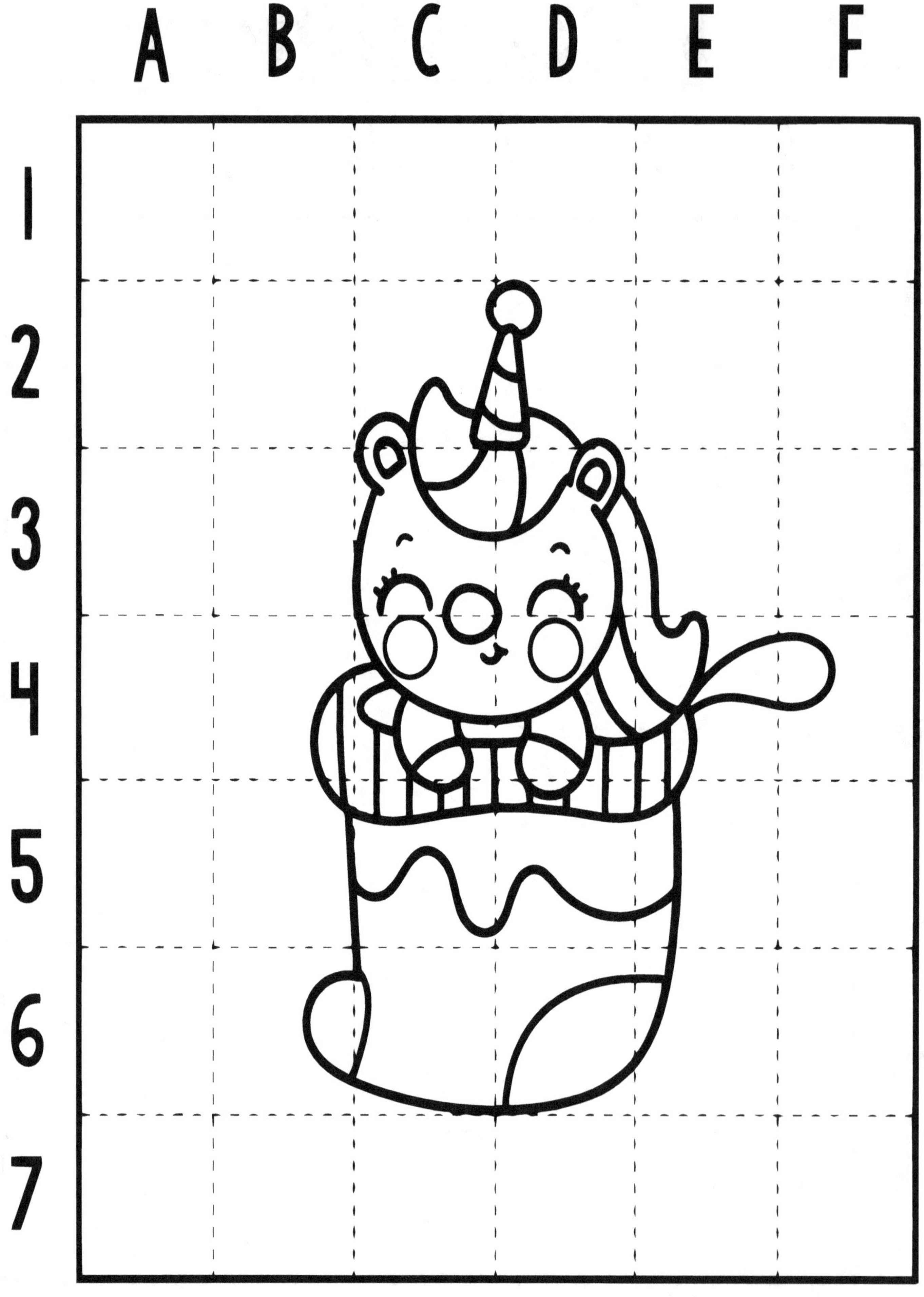
A B C D E F
1
2
3
4
5
6
7

YOUR TURN!

	A	B	C	D	E	F
1						
2						
3						
4						
5						
6						
7						

A B C D E F

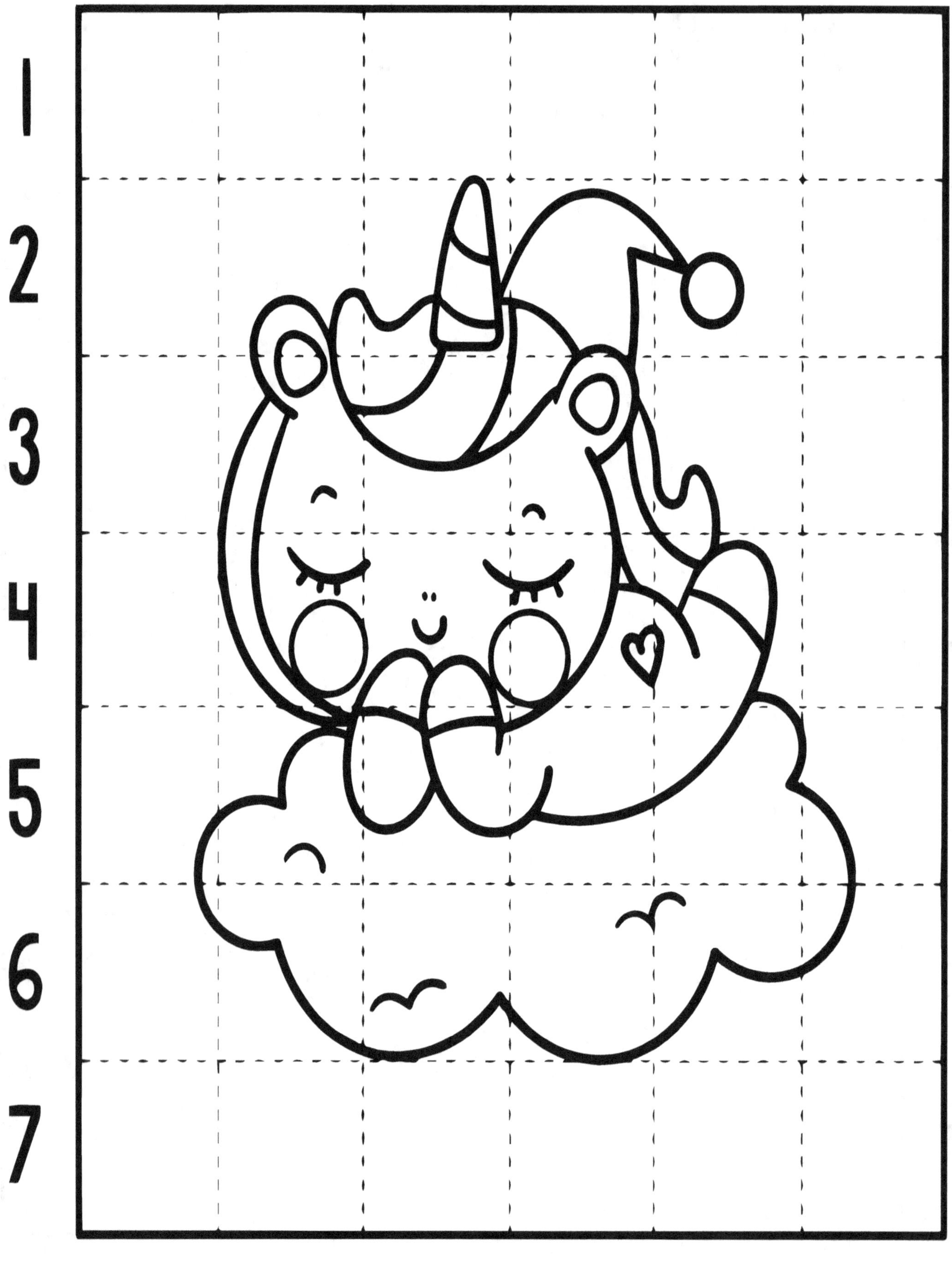

YOUR TURN!

	A	B	C	D	E	F
1						
2						
3						
4						
5						
6						
7						

A B C D E F

1
2
3
4
5
6
7

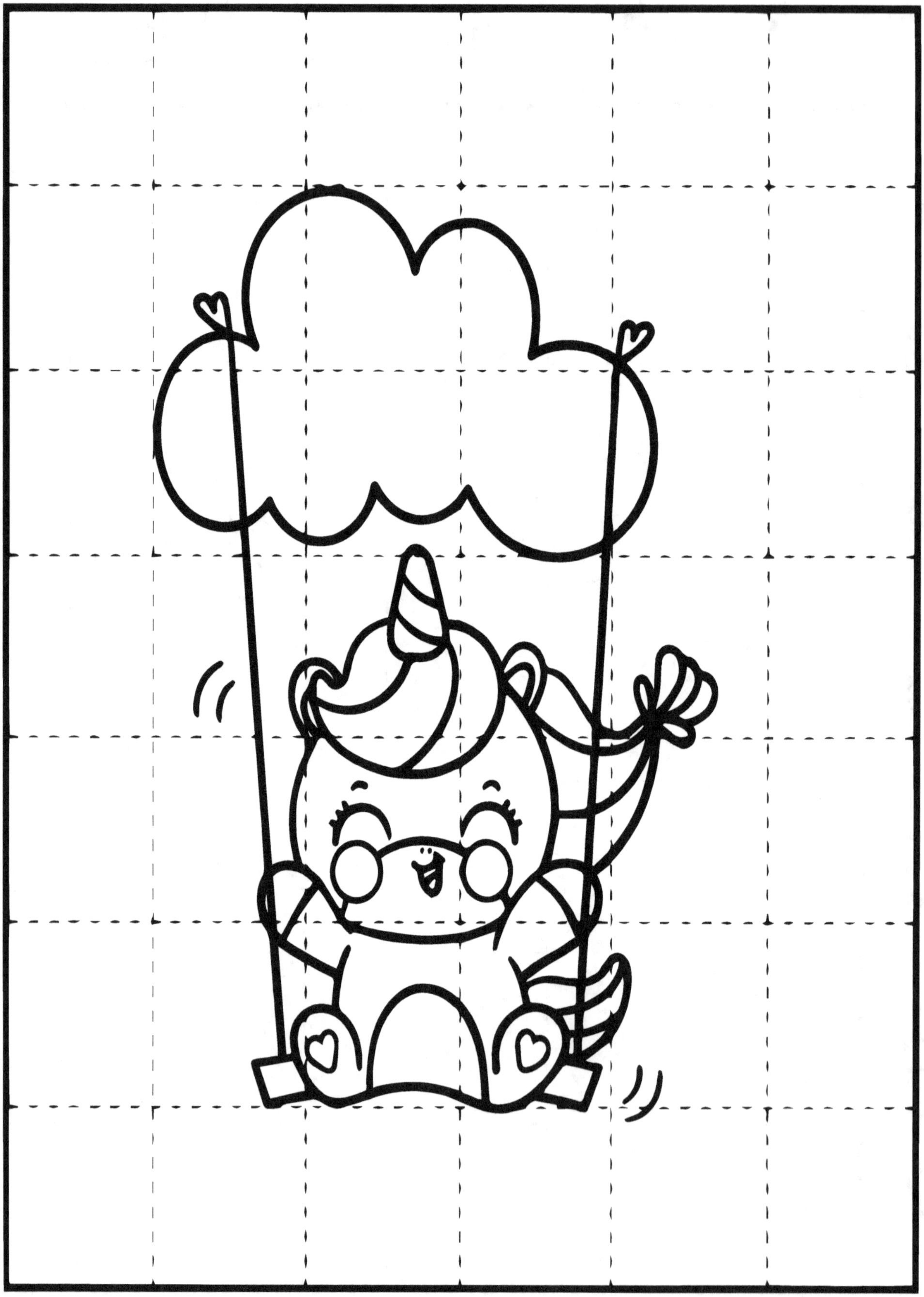

YOUR TURN!

	A	B	C	D	E	F
1						
2						
3						
4						
5						
6						
7						

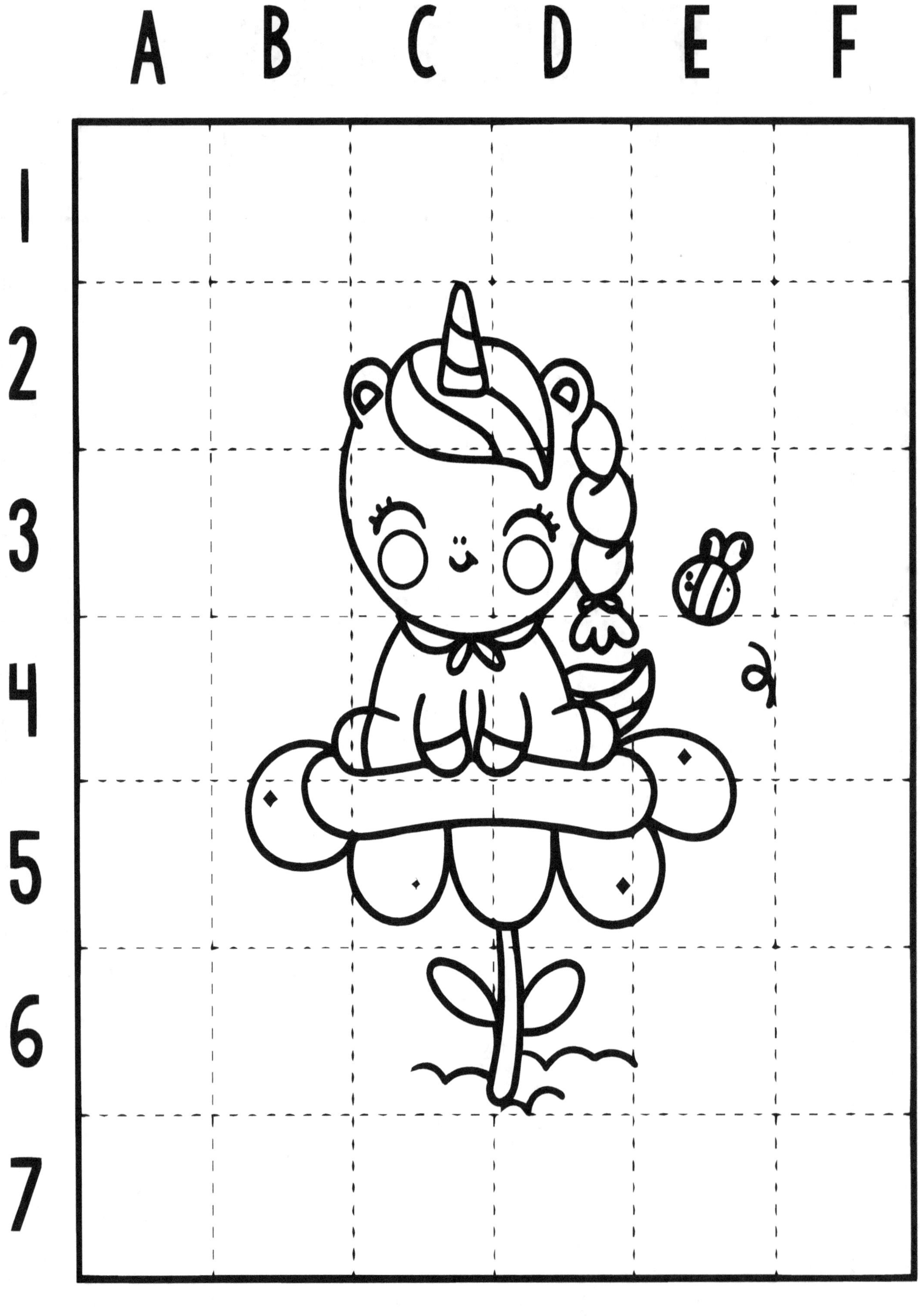
A B C D E F
1
2
3
4
5
6
7

YOUR TURN!

	A	B	C	D	E	F
1						
2						
3						
4						
5						
6						
7						

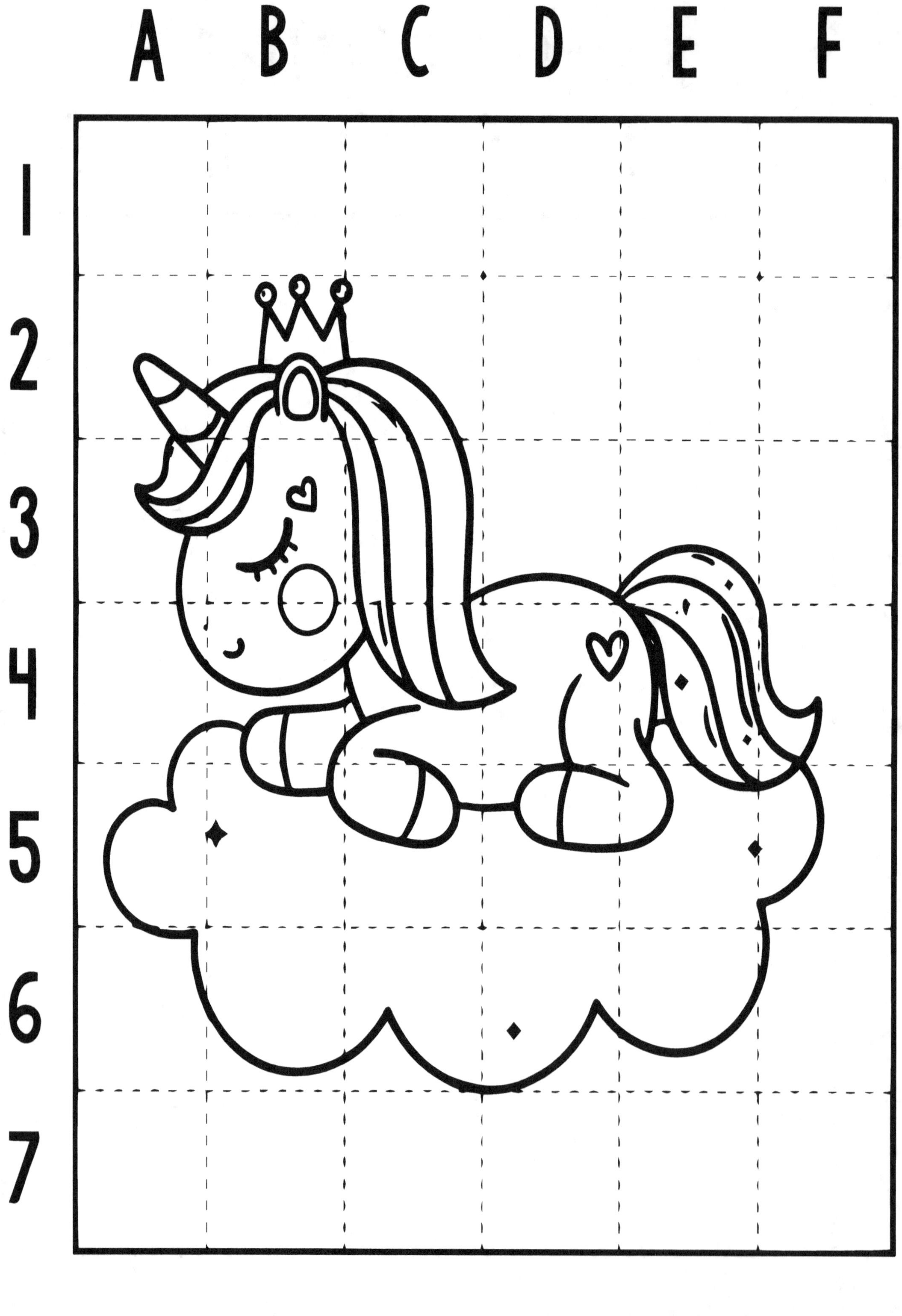
A B C D E F
1
2
3
4
5
6
7

YOUR TURN!

	A	B	C	D	E	F
1						
2						
3						
4						
5						
6						
7						

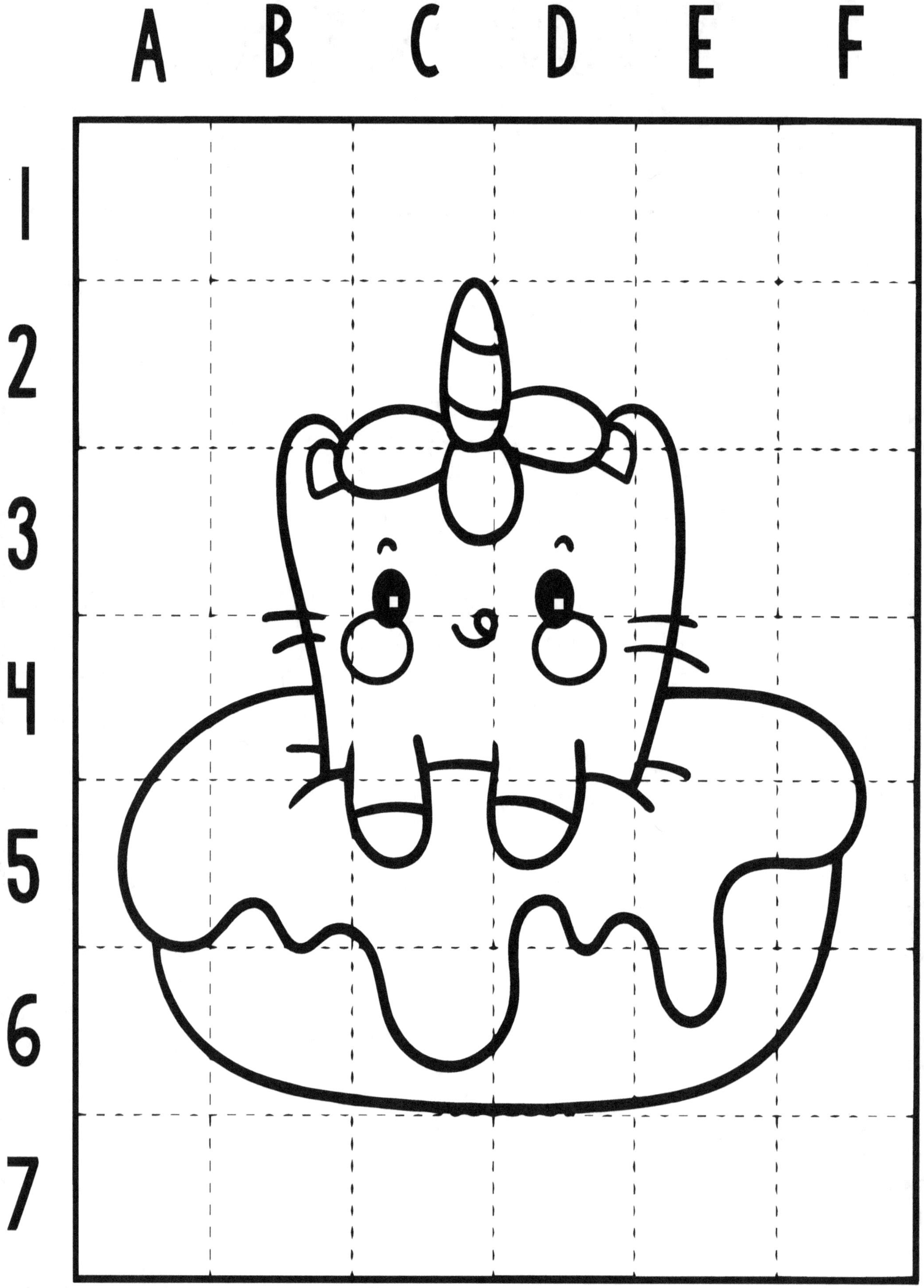
A B C D E F
1
2
3
4
5
6
7

YOUR TURN!

	A	B	C	D	E	F
1						
2						
3						
4						
5						
6						
7						

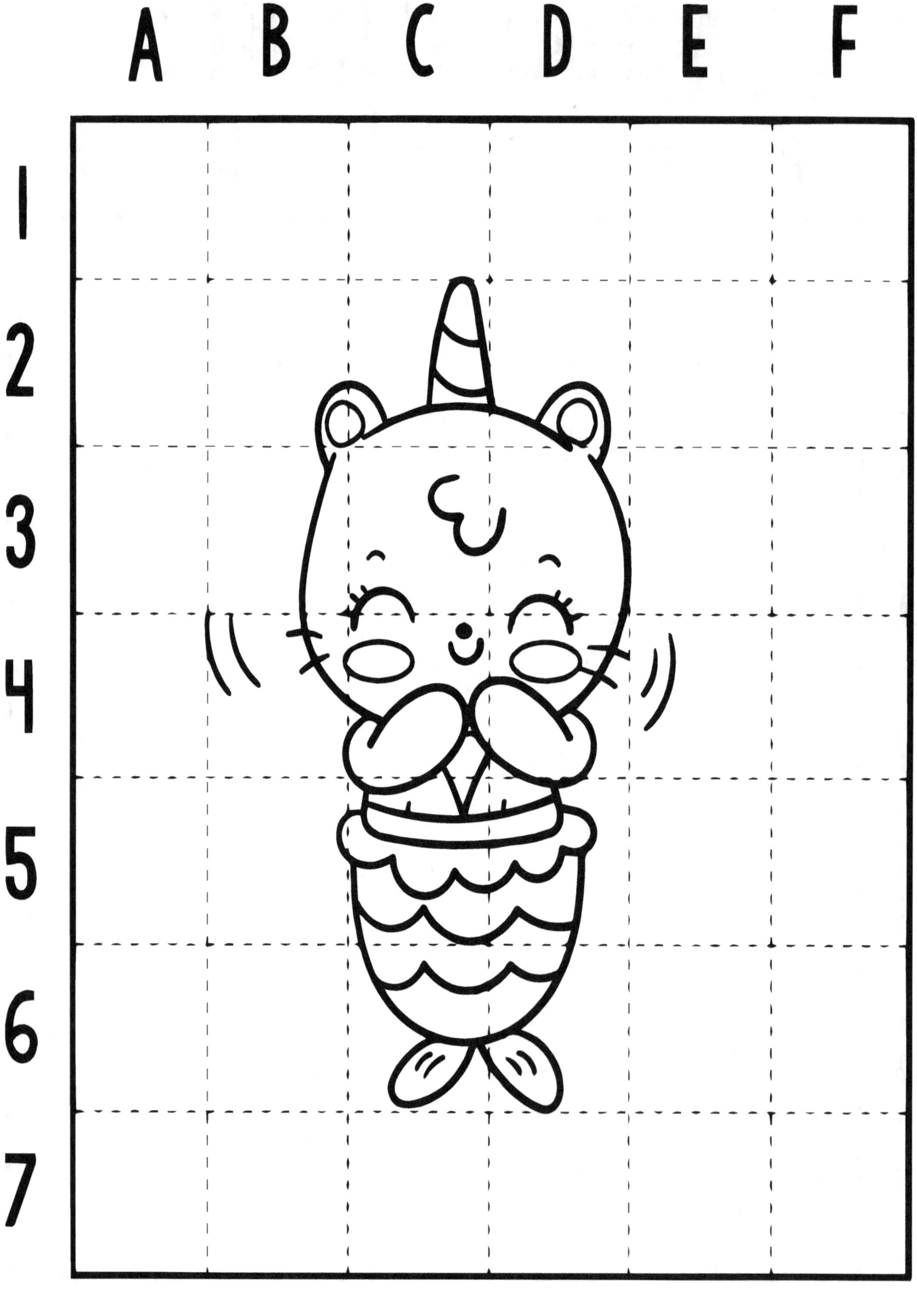
A
B
C
D
E
F
1
2
3
4
5
6
7

YOUR TURN!

	A	B	C	D	E	F
1						
2						
3						
4						
5						
6						
7						

www.ingramcontent.com/pod-product-compliance
Lightning Source LLC
Chambersburg PA
CBHW081441220526
45466CB00008B/2474
* 9 7 9 8 5 7 7 0 5 1 4 4 0 *